Better Homes and Gardens®

STORAGE

BETTER HOMES AND GARDENS® BOOKS

Editor: Gerald M. Knox
Art Director: Ernest Shelton
Managing Editor: David A. Kirchner

Associate Art Directors: Linda Ford Vermie,
Neoma Alt West, Randall Yontz
Copy and Production Editors: Marsha Jahns,
Mary Helen Schiltz, Carl Voss, David A. Walsh
Assistant Art Directors: Harijs Priekulis, Tom Wegner
Senior Graphic Designers: Alisann Dixon, Lynda Haupert,
Lyne Neymeyer
Graphic Designers: Mike Burns, Mike Eagleton, Deb Miner,
Stan Sams, D. Greg Thompson, Darla Whipple, Paul Zimmerman

Vice President, Editorial Director: Doris Eby
Group Editorial Services Director: Duane L. Gregg

General Manager: Fred Stines
Director of Publishing: Robert B. Nelson
Vice President, Retail Marketing: Jamie Martin
Vice President, Direct Marketing: Arthur Heydendael

All About Your House: Storage

Project Editor: James A. Hufnagel
Associate Editor: Willa Rosenblatt Speiser
Assistant Editor: Leonore A. Levy
Copy and Production Editor: Marsha Jahns
Building and Remodeling Editor: Joan McCloskey
Furnishings and Design Editor: Shirley Van Zante
Garden Editor: Douglas A. Jimerson
Money Management and Features Editor: Margaret Daly

Associate Art Director: Linda Ford Vermie
Graphic Designer: Darla Whipple
Electronic Text Processor: Donna Russell

Contributing Editors: Stephen Mead and Jill Abeloe Mead
Contributing Senior Writer: Paul Kitzke
Contributors: Anita Gustafson, Jim Harrold, Cathy Howard,
Jean LemMon

Special thanks to William N. Hopkins, Bill Hopkins, Jr.,
Babs Klein, and Don Wipperman for their valuable
contributions to this book.

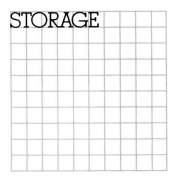

STORAGE

INTRODUCTION

Two things most households never seem to have quite enough of are money and storage. We can't promise that you'll find treasure buried in your basement, but you may very well discover a trove of storage down there, and in almost every other area of your house as well.

Storage tells where to look for it. Family rooms, living rooms, dining rooms, master bedrooms, kids' rooms, kitchens, baths, closets, specialty rooms, even outdoors—this book ranges throughout your house in search of places to put things. Here, you'll find more than 125 examples, all pictured in color, of ways others have eased the storage squeeze at their houses. Drawings, diagrams, and charts tell how you can do the same at yours.

Few homes have totally exhausted their storage potential. But to turn potential into practical, well-organized

reality, you have to take action. Maybe all that's needed are a few hooks or shelves. Maybe you should construct (or have constructed for you) a roomful of built-ins. Or maybe you ought to purchase an instant solution to a storage problem. *Storage* delves into all of these possibilities and helps you analyze which is the best way to go. Then the book provides guidance—everything from dimensions of typical household items to step-by-step how-to-build-it information—that can help you achieve your storage objectives.

We hope that you'll find solutions to more than one of your storage problems in this book. If so, you might also want to take a look at other volumes in the **ALL ABOUT YOUR HOUSE** Library. This comprehensive series of books from Better Homes and Gardens® draws on more than 60 years of experience in helping families bring out the best in their homes.

STORAGE **CONTENTS**

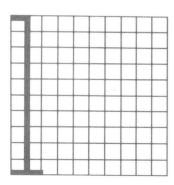

SEEKING OUT THE STORAGE POSSIBILITIES AT YOUR HOUSE

No matter how spacious your home is, you've probably muttered more than once about not having room for everything— or anything, it sometimes seems. Notice we said seems, because in very few homes has every single potential for storage been exploited. Use this chapter as a room-by-room guide to help you analyze the kinds of storage you need and the storage possibilities at your house. When you find a problem that's familiar, or a solution that sounds as though it would work for you, turn to the chapters and pages mentioned for more information.

A living room can be a quiet, formal place, used by adults for conversation and cocktails. Or it can be the center of family activity, playing host to games, television, and children. The kind of living you do in your living room determines the kind of storage you need in it.

If your living room is used for everyday living, chances are it's full of accumulated belongings in need of organization and storage. To help you plan and create neat, unobtrusive living room places for games, video equipment, and the other accessories of daily entertainment, turn to Chapter 2—"Planning Rooms to Maximize Storage."

On the other hand, if your living room is a more serene sort of place, set aside for occasional use, you may have fewer belongings that need to find a home. Books, records, and decorative items are probably the main features, and you may very well want them on display. In the remodeled living room shown here, for example, everything is on view— but instead of predictably flanking the fireplace with banks of shelves, the owners elected to intersperse built-in units with sliding glass doors. Drywalling and painting the bookcases' exteriors blends them into the walls; natural wood interiors pick up the floor's warm tones. Chapter 4—"All About Shelves"—is full of other possibilities.

Good looks are important in all rooms, but often most important in living rooms because they are the most public. If you have unusually attractive collectibles, plants, or art objects, you may want them to double as decoration. If so, Chapter 10—"Storage Surprises"—has some pleasant surprises for you.

IN THE DINING ROOM

The way you use your dining room has a lot to do with the kind of storage you need. If you use it for everyday meals and informal parties, it's almost a part-time family room. If it's reserved for more-formal, less-frequent dinner parties, you may not even think of it as a full-fledged member of the family. Think about how you use your dining room and what it would be useful to store there; then consider what you need at the table and for serving—and we'll give you ideas that will help you customize your dining room storage space as successfully as you would a guest list.

Dining room storage once consisted solely of sideboards, buffets, and corner cupboards. As eating patterns became less formal (and dining rooms smaller), wall units and serving pass-throughs made their debuts.

Particularly if you use your dining room fairly regularly, you'll find that keeping tableware close to where you use it will save you time and energy. Standard freestanding dining room pieces, whether traditional or contemporary in design, can solve storage problems in a hurry. They often provide separate drawers and shelves for table linens, cutlery, and plates—and display space for decorative accessories, too. Many of the ideas in Chapter 5—"Kitchen Storage"—work as well in more-formal settings as they do in the kitchen.

For an uncluttered look that leaves lots of floor space, built-ins are great dining room features. The storage wall shown *at left* provides a focal point for the whole room, as well as ample storage. Dinnerware, linens, and bar supplies all find shelter behind the laminate doors.

This storage unit is light years away from the traditional and still serviceable corner cupboards (complete with small-paned doors and curli-cued pediments) that grace many dining rooms in older homes. It even offers the added convenience of a table-side water source, thanks to a small sink tucked into a recess. For other built-in storage ideas, see Chapter 2.

If wine is an important part of your entertaining, turn to pages 124 and 125 for advice about making or finding space for a wine cellar.

9

SEEKING OUT THE STORAGE POSSIBILITIES AT YOUR HOUSE

IN THE FAMILY ROOM

Family rooms are likely to be all things to all families—informal living rooms, game centers, reading rooms, play-rooms, video centers, even dining rooms. Comfort is the key factor, but it's hard to be comfortable when clutter is at peak levels. If you can find storage space for most of the things that spend most of their time in your family room, you'll be taking a giant step toward enjoying the room more.

The basics of good family room storage aren't hard to plan. A bookshelf and a doored cabinet supporting the television set will give you at least rudimentary storage space. Add a rolltop desk with lots of pigeonholes for bills, checkbook, stamps, and easily misplaced small objects, and you'll be able to make the room look tidy quickly.

But really efficient family room storage should custom-fit your family's life-style. To help you identify the kind of storage you need, consider what your family uses most often. Then decide how many of those items really need to be in the family room, and how accessible they should be.

Are records hard to find, and books piled high on a table meant for evening snacking? Think of purchasing or making an attractive, hard-working shelving system. The custom unit shown *at right* makes especially good use of tall vertical space. Heavy planks span the spaces between window and walls; a rolling library ladder makes everything accessible. Chapter 4—"All About Shelves"—offers more shelving ideas.

If video games and the other electronic gear of twentieth-century entertainment keep getting in the way of traffic patterns and you don't find them attractive enough to store on open shelves, you might put them behind closed cabinet doors. Chapter 3—"Storage Building Basics"—tells how anyone who can build a simple box can add doors to that box and make a cabinet.

IN THE KITCHEN

Food, and the utensils needed to cook and serve it, take up a certain amount of space even if your cooking is in the minimal category. And if you're an accomplished and adventuresome cook who's willing to tackle any recipe that comes your way, kitchen storage can be quite complex. Consider the myriad items you use in preparing even simple meals and you can see that good storage is a key ingredient in the success of any kitchen.

How much storage space you need in your kitchen depends on what kind of cooking you enjoy and how gadget-oriented you are. Fish poachers, woks, steamers, pasta machines, and microwave ovens take up a lot more space than basic pots and pans do. On the other hand, corncob holders, screwdrivers, butter knives, and the other small delights of kitchen gadgetry take up relatively little space. Chapter 5—"Kitchen Storage"—is full of ideas for storing everything from cooking utensils to tableware.

Whether you want to store most of your cookware out in the open or behind closed doors is purely a matter of taste. The owners of the kitchen shown here opted for a combination of both. Drawers and open cabinets in the two islands keep utensils close at hand. Open shelves, shown *below,* were chosen for everyday dishes. Sizing the shelves to suit the items stored there makes a kitchen even more convenient. To learn about sizing shelving spaces and spans, turn to page 63.

Whether you're planning a total kitchen remodeling or just trying to make your existing kitchen work better, cabinet manufacturers and other suppliers offer a wide variety of containers, cupboards, and accessories.

Interested in outdoor cooking? See pages 134 and 135 for some surprising and practical suggestions for backyard kitchens.

IN THE BATH

Does every member of your family use different soaps, different lotions, and assorted cosmetics and electrical appliances—with so much clutter that your main bath looks like a disorganized drugstore? Or are you trying to make more of a small ground-floor guest bath that has barely enough storage room for folded towels? If you organize bath space with storage and convenience as your top priorities, you'll probably be able to accommodate all of the necessities and maybe even some extras.

Because bathrooms are rarely large, and often too small, any storage system that leads two lives is an ideal candidate for bathroom use. The sealed-oak vanity pictured *above,* for example, packs lots of drawers and closed cabinets into the space below. It also provides ample open counter area between and beside the two sinks.

Many baths also have promising dead space. Look around the tub, behind doors, over the toilet—anywhere you find a bit of open space. You can box it in or add shelves to put it to better use. Shelves, in fact, whether open or closed, are naturals in almost any bath.

The sleek, shiny bath/dressing room *opposite* incorporates a shallow, full-length closet behind sliding mirrored panels. The visually space-stretching doors open to reveal space-stretching shelves with lots of room for clothing, towels, and bath accessories.

For more about all kinds of bath storage, from built-ins to purchased accessories, see Chapter 6.

SEEKING OUT THE STORAGE POSSIBILITIES AT YOUR HOUSE

IN THE BEDROOM

Bedrooms are personal domains that often require very personalized storage. Bedding and clothing dimensions are highly standardized, but what about the paraphernalia for a child's hobbies, a teen's stereo system, or an adult's "home work"? The challenge is to organize each bedroom so it's more than just a place to sleep. Here are some suggestions to help wake up the bedrooms at your house.

The bedroom pictured *at right* also serves as an entertainment center and assembly line for a young model-builder. Modular case goods made of plywood and covered with white plastic laminate have the smooth, unobtrusive look of built-ins, but they're actually separate components that can be disassembled; this means the boy could take his room with him years later when he leaves home.

Would different furnishings or built-in units solve bedroom storage problems at your house? Pages 36-39 show how you can plan on paper to maximize storage for master bedrooms. Pages 40-43 do the same for children's rooms.

Hardworking closets
Clothing storage is probably the major, although least-visible, aspect of bedroom storage needs. This means that without considering closets, the bedroom storage story is only half told. Your closets will work harder if you tailor the available space to fit your clothing; pages 100-103 tell how. And if you don't have enough bedroom closets, pages 50 and 51 show how you can construct a new one.

Even more than other rooms, bedrooms often have hidden storage potential. Headboards and bed frames are natural sources for extra shelf or drawer space, and the space under a bed can be put to work, too. To learn about using the space around and under a bed, check pages 52 and 53, and pages 150 and 151.

IN HIDDEN NOOKS AND CRANNIES

Once you've mastered the storage basics for the major rooms of your home, you'll probably need still more space — for seasonal items, for decorative objects, even for everyday things that haven't found a home anywhere else. Then it's time to search for over-looked storage space — over, under, and between whatever is already in place.

Start by looking at every corner of your house that isn't already in use. Look behind doors, under stairs, inside closets, in crawl spaces, below windows—everywhere. You're almost certain to find spaces that aren't living up to their storage potential.

The under-the-eaves office shown *at left* is a lesson on how a little unused space can go a long way. Here, an attic has been transformed from dead storage into a compact and extremely useful work-place. Headroom is limited be-cause of the roof's steep pitch, but clearance is ample for sit-ting, and shelves tuck all the way back into the lowest por-tions of the room, putting every inch to good use.

Stairways to storage
If your attic already is working as hard as it can, how about the stairway leading to it? Or the one that goes down to the basement? Under-stair space is a natural for all sorts of stor-age, from skis to skates to cleaning supplies. Pages 140-142 show ideas for organizing and using space you didn't know you had.

You might find other over-looked storage areas over-head. Pages 144 and 145 show how you can put ceilings to work as storage places.

And then there's storage that's so decorative it doesn't even look like storage—win-dow shelves for small collect-ibles, antique furniture that houses twentieth-century audio equipment, walls hung with three-dimensional art. The more special your needs are, the more interesting possibili-ties you can find; pages 138 and 139 present some intrigu-ing ideas.

SEEKING OUT THE STORAGE POSSIBILITIES AT YOUR HOUSE

OUTDOORS

Sometimes outdoor space is so plentiful it's hard to harness it and use it for something as ordinary as storage. The result is that, for many of us, the garage or basement ends up as a catchall for items that would be much more convenient if they were located elsewhere. Providing good outdoor storage means you don't have to spend a lot of time looking for things and you can enjoy the outdoors more.

Because the outdoor living space at your house is likely to cover more territory than the house itself, where you keep things needs especially careful planning. You don't want to have to walk across the entire property every time you need a trowel.

Tools should be near the garden, mowers near the lawn. If you live in a climate where patio furniture needs to be put away for the winter, try to find storage near your outdoor living room. And necessary but unattractive items such as garbage cans and firewood should be handy to the house but screened from view.

In some cases, mobility is important, too. A wheeled cart that lets you move garden equipment or cooking utensils from the main storage area to the outdoor work center makes sense in all but the smallest yards. If the cart doubles as a storage unit, all the better.

Chapter 9—"Outdoor Storage"—tells how to build carts for both tools and cooking gear; it offers much more, too, about all aspects of outdoor storage, from constructing a simple bicycle rack to building a sizable greenhouse or shed.

A latticework shelter like the one shown *at right* may be an ideal addition to your yard if storage space and shelter from the sun are high priorities. The shelves and counter provide excellent storage for potting materials, and the built-in benches turn it into a pleasant seating area as well. The structure looks complicated at first, but it's basically just three tiers of overlapping decks, topped off with a pair of closets and the latticework.

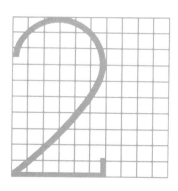

PLANNING ROOMS TO MAXIMIZE STORAGE

If there's an immutable law of homeownership, it's this: All houses shrink, without moving an inch. Week by week, month by month, you're adding an ever-expanding array of objects to a fixed amount of space. At first, you store them easily. Later, you cram them in wherever you can. Finally, you may begin to feel like giving up and moving to a larger house. A more sensible solution is to stay put and make better use of the space you have. This chapter presents a room-by-room guide to planning storage systems that can take care of everything you own without taking over your house at the same time.

In general, good storage systems provide places for everything and encourage you to keep your household neat and organized. This, of course, is easier said than done, especially when you're faced with the wide variety of items every home has to house. Fortunately, you can buy or build enough different types of storage to accommodate almost anything.

Plan ahead
Before you buy or build anything, size up the situation. First, compile a list of all the objects you want or need to store in each of your home's living areas. Kitchens and baths are the likeliest places to start (see Chapters 5 and 6 for more detailed information about these two rooms). Make similar notes for your living room, dining room, family room, and bedrooms—the subjects of this chapter.

As you work, think about your family's habits and styles of living. Plan to store items such as books, records, games, camera equipment, and sports gear where the people who use them most can find them without turning the room upside down.

Next, ask yourself *why* you need storage. The most important reasons are to get the things you own out of the way, protect them, and make them simpler to locate. Yet storage can serve other purposes at the same time. With the right system, you can create extra floor space, unclutter a room, even add a decorating focal point to the entire area.

Once you know what you plan to store and where, it's time to match your possessions to storage units that most adequately suit your needs,

taste, and budget. Cabinets and bookshelves aren't the only options—far from it. In fact, your choices are almost unlimited: modular units, bunching or stacking pieces, freestanding storage systems, built-in designs, and multifunctional units, to name only a few.

Helpful definitions
As you're planning, think of space in relation to the kinds of objects you intend to store, how often you need them, and how visible and easy-to-get-at you want them to be.
• *Live*—that is, easily accessible—storage space should be reserved for items you use nearly every day. Bookshelves in a living room, cupboards in a dining room, and multipurpose units in a family room or bedroom are good examples.
• *Occasional* storage space is for those items you retrieve to put into use at set times of the year, such as Christmas tree stands, rakes, skis, and baseball gloves.
• *Dead* storage space is for things you rarely need but don't want to discard (and don't want to display, either). Unoccupied or out-of-the-way areas of the house like the attic, garage, or basement are ideal for dead storage.

All types of storage can be either *open* or *closed*. Open systems—generally shelves of one kind or another—permit you to display your most attractive possessions. In addition, they make more mundane objects easier to get at.

Cabinets and closets are typical closed storage units. They're better than open storage at protecting the things you own, and at hiding a temporary mess until you have a chance to really get organized.

LIVING ROOMS

Planning storage for a living room is no easy task. After all, the area is meant for *living*, not for stowing every item you can think of. Nevertheless, it's also a room for displaying some of the best, most attractive things you own—books, collectibles, decorative accessories—in or on storage units that are equally pleasing to the eye. The key, then, is to devise solutions that are both space-stretching and good-looking.

In many living rooms, floor space is a precious commodity. If it is in yours, try building up, not out. Use space along a wall, and stack ready-made storage pieces—drawers, cabinets, shelves—from floor to ceiling. Or build a whole wall of storage on your own. You can even save on floor space entirely by installing wall-mounted cabinets or shelves.

Many living rooms also have quirky little angles or jogs in one or more walls. Put this wasted space to work with freestanding or built-in shelves.

Look closely at other parts of the room, as well. The area surrounding a window or fireplace is often prime territory for a built-in unit. Properly designed, it can serve both as storage and as an eye-catching focal point in the room.

At the same time, evaluate the space directly in front of a window. You may be able to fill it with an extra seating piece that also has doors or drawers.

Shelf life
Books are a wonderful sight to see and add strong decorating appeal to even the most formal living room. When you think of storing books, keep a few general principles in mind.

Start by estimating the shelf space you'll need. Eight to 10 hardbound books or 12 to 14 paperbacks usually take up about a foot of shelf.

Books aren't the only things that go on shelves. All sorts of collectibles or accessories pose similar storage challenges. As you're planning, remember that all collections tend to grow and grow and then grow some more. Allow space for new acquisitions. Consider, too, that displays of many similar items, impressive though they may be, are less interesting and appealing to the eye than mixed groups.

The number and size of items in a collection should determine the kinds of shelves that will fit in best. If you have a large collection, think about using an entire wall at one end of the room for permanent shelving. Or, take up wall space with adjustable shelf standards and brackets, and add sections as your collection expands.

If you have relatively few books or other collected items, a single piece of furniture may be the answer. Buy a bookcase or build one yourself (see Chapters 3 and 4).

Finally, don't neglect more unusual solutions. For example, you may be able to hang smaller shelves high on the walls, opening up the area below for seating.

Sample layout
Perhaps more than in any other area of the house, storage units in the living room must match the rest of your decor. The arrangement pictured *at right* represents one approach you could take to outfitting a living room with different kinds of storage, complemented by a particular fabric, carpeting, and color.

(continued)

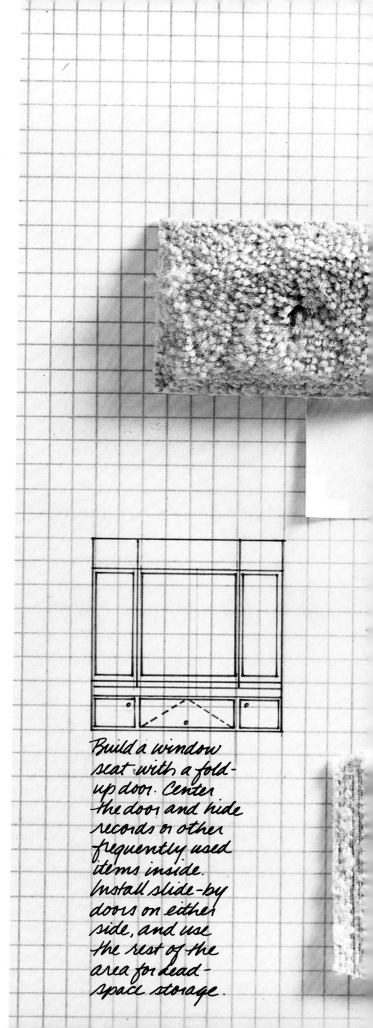

Build a window seat with a fold-up door. Center the door and hide records or other frequently used items inside. Install slide-by doors on either side, and use the rest of the area for dead-space storage.

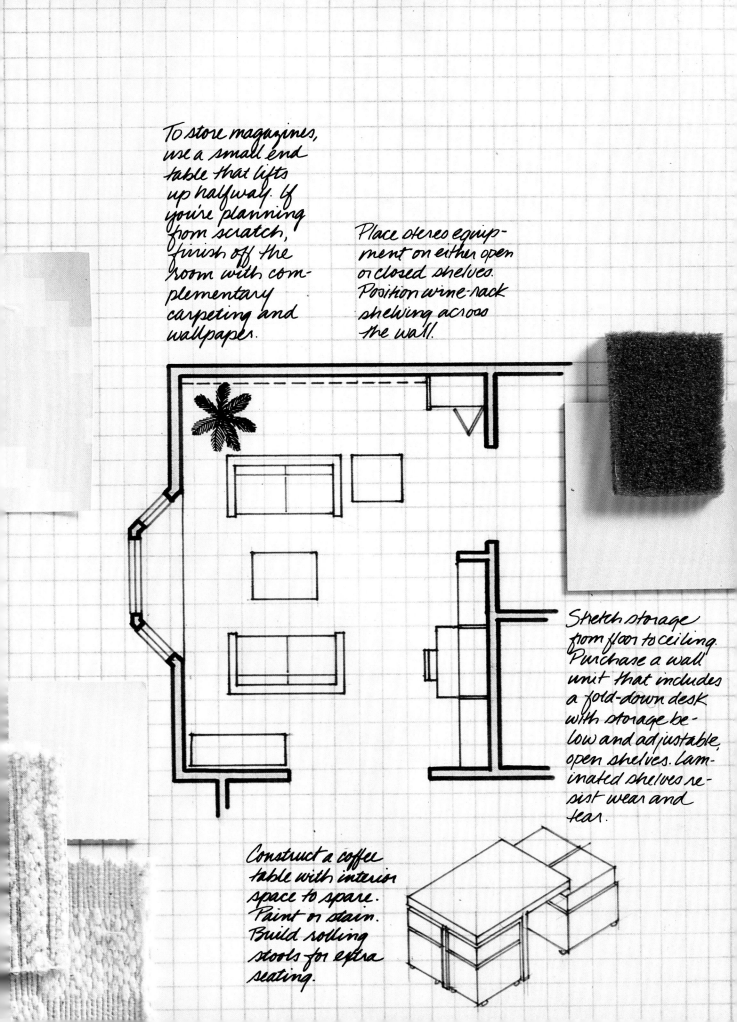

To store magazines, use a small end table that lifts up halfway. If you're planning from scratch, finish off the room with complementary carpeting and wallpaper.

Place stereo equipment on either open or closed shelves. Position wine-rack shelving across the wall.

Stretch storage from floor to ceiling. Purchase a wall unit that includes a fold-down desk with storage below and adjustable, open shelves. Laminated shelves resist wear and tear.

Construct a coffee table with interior space to spare. Paint or stain. Build rolling stools for extra seating.

LIVING ROOMS
(continued)

Whether you build or buy them, good storage units are multi-purpose marvels, made to do more than one thing. Here are several examples that can work well in most living rooms.

• Ready-made shelves, complete with drawers, can run along an entire wall. Install them high enough to leave room for movable seating pieces below.

• Modular storage furniture can serve as comfortable seating and is easy to rearrange.

• Freestanding wall units, which you can assemble yourself, offer enough different kinds of storage—open and closed shelves, cabinets, and drawers—to accommodate diverse items.

• Rolling, easily built storage carts house cocktail glasses and accessories; commercially available models have folding shelves that open into one or more serving trays.

If you're lucky enough to have a fireplace, do you also have a place to keep wood? One solution is to buy a specially designed storage cabinet, one that's lined with metal or tile. Install it next to the fireplace, and keep a week's supply right at your fingertips. If the cabinet is on an exterior wall, you can provide a door for loading it from the outside, as long as the opening conforms to local building codes.

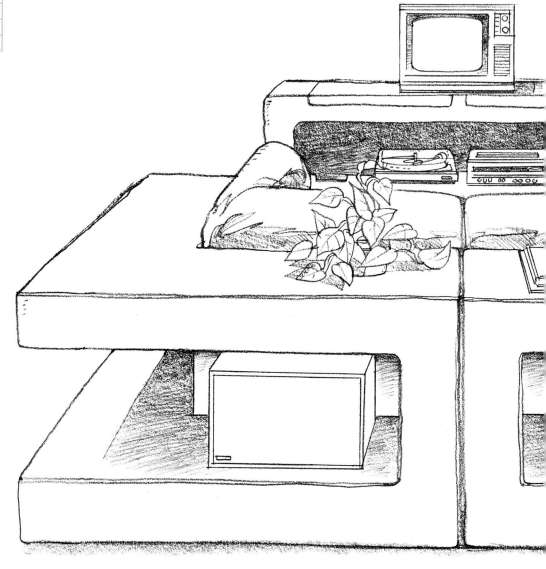

The most efficient living room layouts have furniture pieces that do more than one job; they can deliver decorating appeal, add surface area, and provide storage. The coffee table illustrated at left is a good example. With the two sliding sections together, it's a good-looking wooden unit that has plenty of space on top. Moved apart, the sections reveal a box with enough room for glassware, ashtrays, coasters, or a range of other items, including table games.

When a living room is also a media center, custom storage is often the best approach. The sectional units pictured at left have spaces specifically sized for video equipment, stereo components, albums, tapes, and other electronic gear. Two of the sections also serve as built-in seating pieces.

The space on either side of a fireplace is a likely spot for the kind of built-in shelving illustrated above. Shelves of varying heights can accommodate books of different sizes, with hide-away accessories stored in a floor-level cabinet.

The inexpensive, easily built project shown at right is a model of versatility. Open, it's a writing desk, with large drawers that can hold files, folders, even small pieces of office equipment. The side shelves provide extra room for books and supplies. When it's not see-ing active duty, the writing surface folds down and the whole unit closes up to be-come an attractive cabinet that fits into most living room schemes. Casters make the unit easy to move from one spot to another.

DINING ROOMS

Practicality counts in every dining room—even the most formal one. Though you'll probably want to display fine dishes and glassware for all to see, don't forget that storage is not primarily a decorative art. Place serving pieces, china, and other items within easy reach, but make sure they're well protected against accidents and children's curiosity.

For best display, use open shelves. Position them high enough so objects aren't in line with errant elbows, but not so high that you can't see objects clearly or dust them easily. One way to make open units safer is to add a lip along the edge of each shelf. Another is to allow a 1-inch margin between stored items and the edge of the shelf.

Closed cabinets, with glass or plastic doors, are a little less effective as display storage. Even so, they're better at protecting objects and keeping them free of dust.

Piece by piece

Try to make or buy units that are equal in dimensions to the dinnerware you plan to store. Shelves 12 inches deep should hold all but the largest serving pieces. Also, remember that unlike most items, plates lend themselves to stacking; don't hesitate to store them one atop the other.

If you're really short on space or aren't interested in display storage, think about using easy-to-install pullout shelves. They're available in different materials and match up well with most cabinets. Vertical units, such as inexpensive wire or plastic racks, are also simple, space-saving options that look good in the right setting. Stack larger pieces on

16-inch shelves or, for better display, use tilted shelving on a 12- to 14-inch base.

Unlike flatware, cups don't stack very efficiently. Try storing them one-deep on half-shelves. Or hang them on sliding racks in a cabinet or out of the way on hooks installed under a cabinet shelf.

The main problem with storing glasses is arranging them so you can quickly get at each one without risking a shattering experience every day. Don't use deep storage; instead, place glasses near the front of shallower shelves. Adjustable shelving will help cut down on wasted space and allow you to store different sets of glasses efficiently in even a relatively small cabinet.

You also might consider attaching half-shelves at the back of a cabinet, placing plates below and easy-to-get-at glasses above.

Lay away linens

Tablecloths and napkins should be wrinkle-free and readily accessible. If you pile them together, they won't be. As one option, consider storing each set separately on adjustable or pullout shelving placed in a closet or cabinet. Movable racks, also installed in a closet or cabinet, are effective alternatives, as are large drawers below a buffet.

The arrangement shown *at right* is one way you could set up a dining area to take care of all your storage needs and still have plenty of room left for the main business of eating and entertaining. It includes both closed and open storage—some fixed, some mobile. Combined with complementary finishes and carpeting, it's a flexible, functional layout that both conserves and creates space.

(continued)

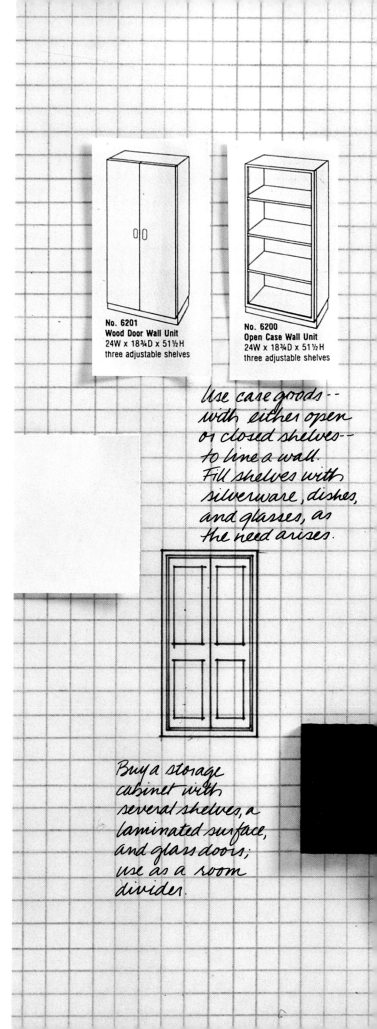

No. 6201
Wood Door Wall Unit
24W x 18¾D x 51½H
three adjustable shelves

No. 6200
Open Case Wall Unit
24W x 18¾D x 51½H
three adjustable shelves

Use case goods -- with either open or closed shelves -- to line a wall. Fill shelves with silverware, dishes, and glasses, as the need arises.

Buy a storage cabinet with several shelves, a laminated surface, and glass doors; use as a room divider.

Let a server do triple duty. Build one with room for storage, and add casters so you can roll it to where it's most needed.

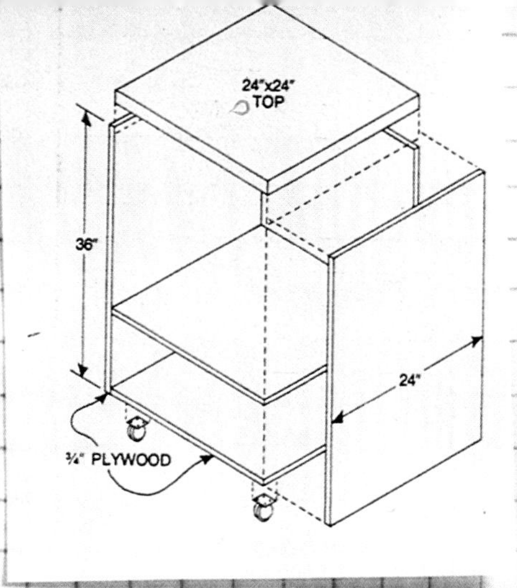

24"x24"
TOP

36"

24"

¾" PLYWOOD

Turn a wall, windowed or not, into one of the hardest-working parts of your home. Place storage units along it, either flanking a window or with a shelf centered between two units on a room-length wall. Allow drawer space below the buffet for storing table linens. Cover all surfaces with laminate.

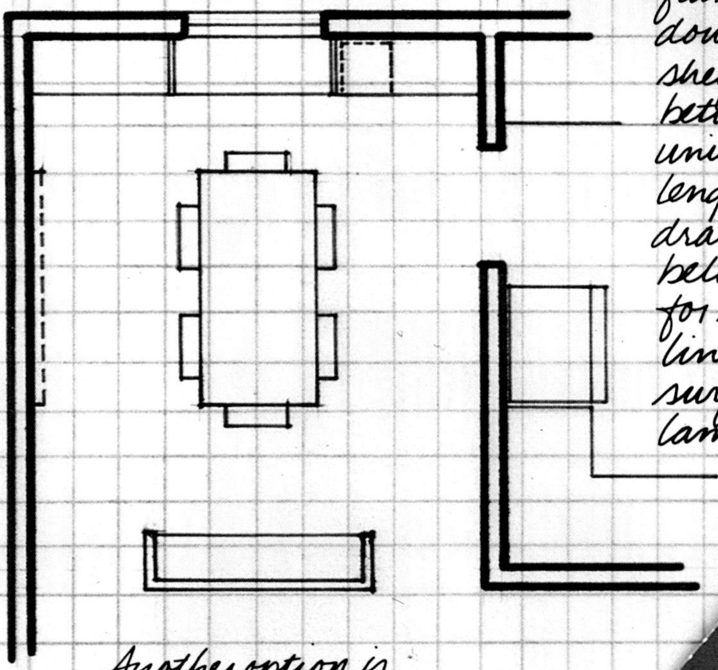

Keep a handy rack on the wall for easy access to serving pieces.

Another option is to build a storage divider from particle-board and laminate. Install casters for mobility.

DINING ROOMS
(continued)

How to stock a dining room with storage pieces depends on the area's size, its relationship to the rest of the house, and the number of other activities it has to cater to. Keep these tips in mind.

• If you have a large room reserved only for dining, a wall of built-in storage is an appealing way to show off the whole area. A combination of cabinets, drawers, and shelves provides plenty of open and closed space for different items to be easily accessible and neatly separated.

• The tiniest dining room can be well served by only a few simply built wall-hung shelves. Using brackets, you can install them in a matter of minutes. Painted or stained, they add inexpensive decorating appeal to the room.

• If the dining area has to do double duty or you often eat in other rooms, think about including one or more pieces of movable storage. You can buy or build mobile chests, buffets, serving carts, even refrigerators. Many of these units, in addition to housing glassware, tableware, and linens, have pop-up or folding shelves to provide extra surface space.

• Don't always play it straight, either. Combine storage systems by installing wall-hung cabinets and shelves that are designed to bend around a corner, between the living room and dining area, for example. On one side, you can store books, stereo components, and collectibles; on the other, a full complement of conventional dinnerware.

• Informal eating areas are often play or work spaces, as well. If yours fits this description, consider using built-in or freestanding seating pieces with storage bins or drawers to shelter nondining items.

Well-made, handcrafted reproductions of classic furniture pieces, like the corner cupboard illustrated above, can add a stately, architectural look to most dining rooms without taking up a lot of floor space. For all its fine-lined old-fash- **ioned beauty, however, it also satisfies thoroughly modern storage needs. The deep, open shelves are ideal for displaying the family's best china and pewter; closed shelves below can house silverware, glassware, or table linens.**

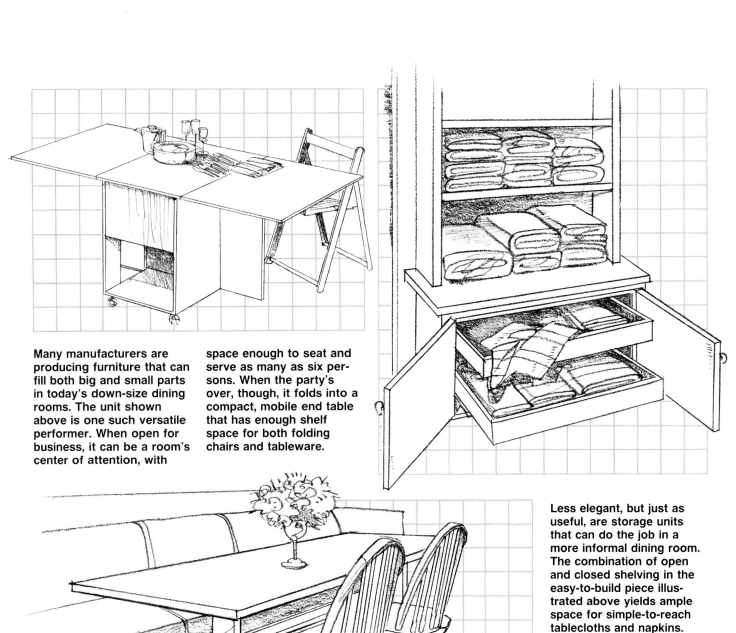

Many manufacturers are producing furniture that can fill both big and small parts in today's down-size dining rooms. The unit shown above is one such versatile performer. When open for business, it can be a room's center of attention, with space enough to seat and serve as many as six persons. When the party's over, though, it folds into a compact, mobile end table that has enough shelf space for both folding chairs and tableware.

Less elegant, but just as useful, are storage units that can do the job in a more informal dining room. The combination of open and closed shelving in the easy-to-build piece illustrated above yields ample space for simple-to-reach tablecloths and napkins.

Two-in-one designs pack a big storage punch when space is sparse. Below each end of the banquette, shown at left, are pullout bins large enough to house dining room accessories of all kinds. Similar units feature lift-up tops for equally easy access.

31

FAMILY ROOMS

To be flexible enough to handle the needs of everyone from toddlers to teens to parents and their guests, family room storage should be both abundant and versatile. How you use some kinds of units—simple bookcases or shelves, for example—will parallel the way you might arrange them in your living room (see pages 24 and 25). For the most part, however, storage in a family room should be less suited to single purposes and more adaptably utilitarian.

What goes where?

When you start planning, first consider all of the items you'll have to store. The list probably will include books, games, hobby and office supplies, a television set, stereo and electronic equipment, record albums, and even small pieces of knockdown furniture. As the list grows, it's a good idea to generously overestimate the amount of storage space you'll need. The additional space will disappear quickly.

Using closed, built-in storage walls is one approach that will allow you to change the environment to suit the occasion. When the area's concealed behind attractively designed doors, you can use the room for adult entertaining. When the doors are open, exposing a television set, games, and toys, the atmosphere changes, and the room becomes a perfect spot for the younger set.

Placed along a wall, freestanding cabinets and shelves can accomplish the same objectives. Set perpendicular to a wall, these units make excellent room dividers.

Every family room needs at least one table for games, snacks, homework, or hobbies, or simply as a useful place to temporarily stack

things. You can buy or build them with storage compartments. In most cases, however, the best type of table for a family room, where you often require floor space at a moment's notice, is one that can be folded up and stashed away.

Even more important is comfortable seating, which you can build in, with storage bins or drawers installed below. Modular sofas are another option. Individual sections can be positioned wherever they fit best and then easily moved if necessary. Arrange them in an L-shape, and place them in a corner. Or make the sections part of an integrated storage system by attaching wall-hung cabinets or shelves to them. To be most useful, each module should have closed storage beneath and maybe even a backboard that's large enough to provide extra surface space.

Electronic media

In addition to the standard television set and stereo system, contemporary family rooms are likely to have other types of electronic gear. Freestanding cabinets and shelves can handle most of these items, as can changeable storage modules. Inexpensive movable carts will accommodate portable TVs or cassette players. And if you're a really serious buff, house all the equipment on built-in shelves hidden from view by folding doors.

In the room arrangement shown here, built-in wall units and modular seating, enhanced by cool colors and durable surfaces, provide a lot of storage with plenty of floor space left over.

(continued)

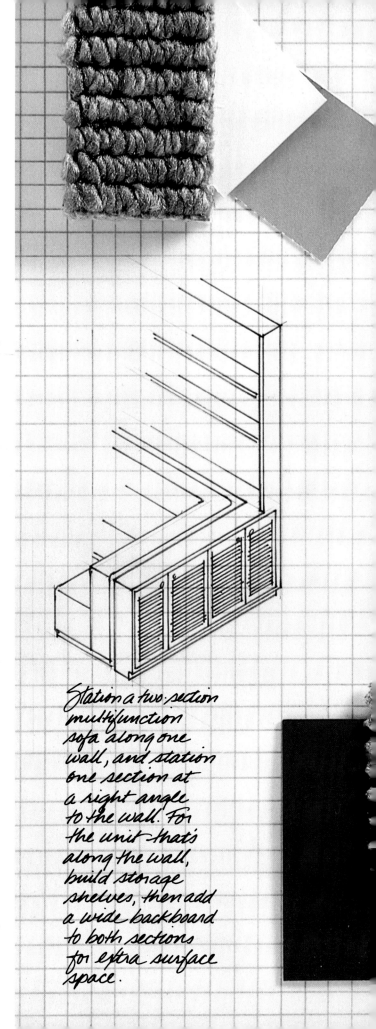

Station a two-section multifunction sofa along one wall, and station one section at a right angle to the wall. For the unit that's along the wall, build storage shelves, then add a wide backboard to both sections for extra surface space.

Use a foldaway
game or dining
table that you
can store inside
the wall unit
when you want
to clear more floor
space.

Don't leave a desk
standing all
alone. Frame the
unit with floor-
to-ceiling shelves,
and add shelves
above the desk
as well.

The fabric-covered
sofa in this room
arrangement
has storage space
nearly everywhere.
Its backboard is
almost tabletop
wide, with room
for a potpourri
of different
objects. Use the
area below each
seating piece
for bins or
drawers.

Reserve the area
at the end of the
wall unit for
closed storage.
Shuttered doors
are a good touch
in a family
room.

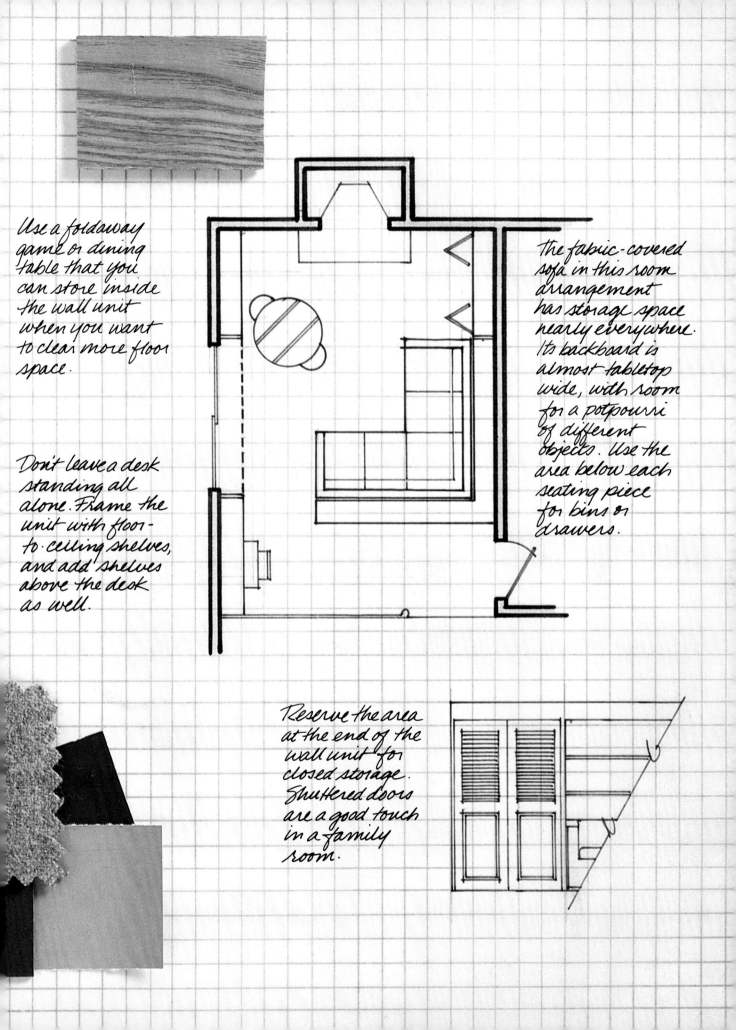

FAMILY ROOMS

(continued)

Without ample storage space, a family room can quickly go from cozy to cluttered, littered with every household item imaginable. Here are some suggestions that can help keep things in their place.

• As in other rooms of the house, built-in storage—whole walls of shelves, cabinets, and drawers—is often a logical choice. It's the single best way to design from scratch systems that most nearly match the needs—and possessions—of everyone in your family. Moreover, built-ins are undeniably effective at transforming a homely room into a stunning beauty, without taking up much, if any, floor space.

• Once built-ins are added, they're there for good. Modular storage units, however, which come in myriad sizes, shapes, and materials, are made for the peripatetic decorator: They're easy to change and rearrange. You can find modular pieces for every family room function, including adjustable-shelf bookcases, vertically slotted record holders, pigeonholes for cassettes, deep units for television sets, racks for wine bottles, and models designed for desk or bar service. And modulars are sold as finished furniture, unfinished units, or unassembled sections you can put together yourself.

• If your budget's tight, don't neglect build-it-yourself solutions. Wall-hung shelves and freestanding bookcases, for example, are projects most amateur furniture-makers can tackle successfully. In addition, think about using things you already own in novel ways. Two possibilities are: retired kitchen cabinets called to active duty in the family room and a long-forgotten armoire adapted to hold stereo components.

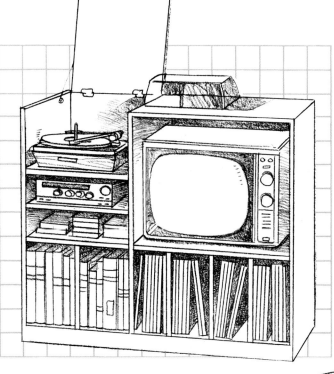

When space is short and money tight, a simple-to-put-together plywood storage case like the one pictured at left is a hard-working place to house everything from a television set to stereo components to record albums and books. The key to this kind of display storage is its carefully measured shelving; each section is precisely designed to accommodate specific items. And although the compartments themselves are stationary, the entire unit needn't be. Simply add casters and the unit can roll wherever it's needed most.

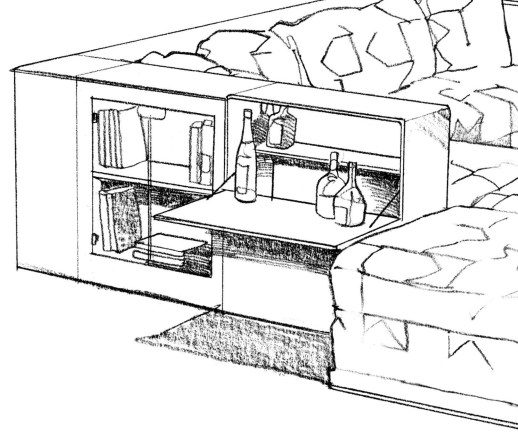

Freestanding, multipurpose storage units are popular in family rooms everywhere. Attractive pieces that combine cabinets and drawers come in all shapes and sizes and can be moved from room to room or home to home with a minimum of effort. If they're finished on the back as well, they also can double as room dividers. The hardworking armoire illustrated below is especially flexible. The space-saving bifold doors open to reveal shelves of various heights, ideal for storing a wide range of objects. The television set sits on a swivel shelf, and the pullout laminate surface is a bartender's delight.

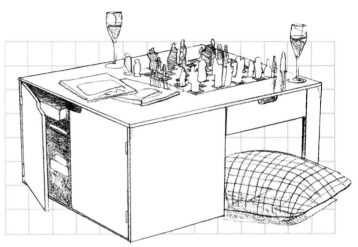

Ready-made storage is fine, but do-it-yourself units also can fill the bill. Easily built plywood coffee tables, like the one shown above, are all a game player really needs. The large surface yields plenty of room to spread out, and the spacious cabinets and a drawer keep items out of sight between games. Part of the top can be constructed so that it flips over—one side plain, the other a painted chessboard.

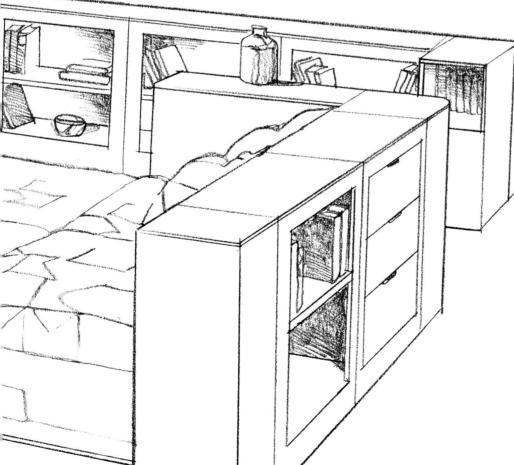

Few other storage solutions can match the adaptability of modular furniture. With the versatile units shown at left, a room arrangement can grow piece by piece, perfect for a family with changing needs and a limited budget. At the same time, modular systems are a decorator's dream: They can be seating pieces, storage pieces, or a combination of both, and can fit uncommonly well into more than one room and even more than one home. The group of units illustrated here looks complex, but it's really not. Coordinated with sectional seating, this storage system—a spacious array of shelves, drawers, and cabinets—can accommodate books, glasses, games, collectibles, and more, all in one attractively open pattern.

35

MASTER BEDROOMS

Not so long ago, the main bedroom was a quiet way station, little more than a spot to sleep and hide away clothes. It had a bed, one or two dressers, and a closet. Times have changed. Instead of being a sleepily inactive part of the house, today's master bedroom is just as likely to be a secondary living area, complete with books, television set, stereo system, even exercise equipment. Of course, you still need space for a bed and clothes storage, so the question becomes: How do you put everything in its place and still make the place look good?

Modular makeup

One of the most efficient ways to arrange furniture in a bedroom, including storage pieces, is to take a modular approach to the problem. Use a series of small units, rather than a few large ones. Group them in a flexible layout that permits you to create individual areas for different purposes. Then, when you want a change of space, all you have to do is regroup the units.

Most important, make a single piece do double or even triple duty. For instance, one ordinary cabinet can serve as a room divider and, at the same time, provide a space-saving combination of storage, display, and work surfaces.

Advice that adds up

As you're planning, consider one, two, or more of these specific suggestions for storing items in a master bedroom.
• Make use of space under the bed. Buy or build a movable plinth, and stash away blankets and bed linens there.
• Arrange all the storage units in a small bedroom along one wall, leaving the rest of the room for the bed and maybe

a chair or two. Use several pieces—cabinets, shelves, drawers, and dressing table.
• Add a large headboard, properly matched to the bed and other furniture in the room. If it has several low shelves, you can use them as a combination night table and bookcase, saving floor space in the process.
• Small rooms with small pieces of furniture tend to look even smaller than they are. If your bedroom is truly tiny, stretch the space with built-ins. Strip the area to bare essentials—perhaps only a double bed and chair—and then get storage room by making the walls work as hard as possible: Custom-built wardrobes and closed shelves may be your best bets.

Into the closet

Relatively small changes in a standard closet can yield a bonanza of new storage space.

For example, most doors don't extend all the way from floor to ceiling. By enlarging the opening and installing a taller door, you'll make the area at the top of the closet much more accessible.

Further, many doors don't expose the closet's full width, which leaves dead space on either side. To get at it, widen the doorway and put in doors that open across the entire width. Install bifold or sliding doors, which take up a minimum of floor space.

No single part of the room arrangement shown *at right* is wildly unconventional, but taken together, the storage units add up to uncommonly abundant space. The headboard and bedside pieces are especially practical, and the colors and patterns of carpeting, bedspread, and wallpaper are brightly space-enhancing.

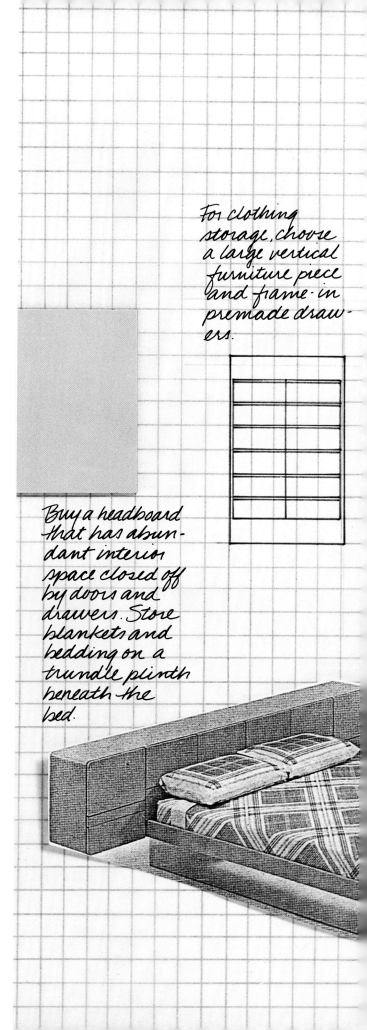

For clothing storage, choose a large vertical furniture piece and frame-in premade drawers.

Buy a headboard that has abundant interior space closed off by doors and drawers. Store blankets and bedding on a trundle plinth beneath the bed.

(continued)

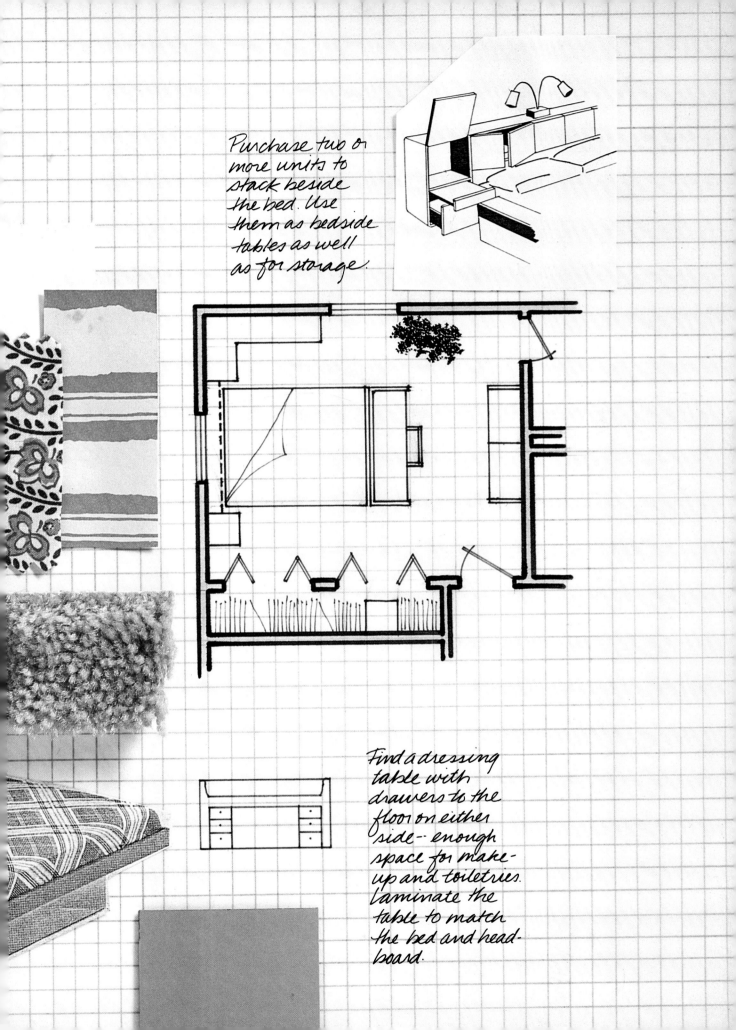

Purchase two or
more units to
stack beside
the bed. Use
them as bedside
tables as well
as for storage.

Find a dressing
table with
drawers to the
floor on either
side -- enough
space for make-
up and toiletries.
Laminate the
table to match
the bed and head-
board.

MASTER BEDROOMS

(continued)

Don't let storage problems catch you napping. Try one or more of these buy-it or build-it ideas.

• In a large bedroom, consider installing a big double headboard with open shelves for display storage. The headboard also can serve as a divider. Take it a step further by placing individual dressers on either side of the bed to create two separate grooming areas.

• Revamp your closets. No matter how large they are, too often they have too much wasted space. By employing a combination of different-size drawers and shelves, you can store all your clothes in the *entire* area from floor to ceiling and still have room for suitcases, travel bags, and other articles.

• Even the best-organized closet needs help if it's just too small to begin with. When the squeeze is on in your bedroom, think about building a large, freestanding wardrobe, with a central compartment for hanging clothes. Add deep cabinets above and drawers below the compartment.

• Another inexpensive, easy-to-build project for an active bedroom is a set of long, low plywood boxes stacked along a wall to any height you wish. By adding sliding doors and a drop-down desk, you not only create a spacious storage case, but a work area as well.

• If your master suite includes a bath, buy or build a linen closet outfitted with storage compartments specifically designed for various kinds of items: pullout trays for washcloths, sheets, pillowcases, and towels; deep shelves for blankets and bedding; and shallow shelves and drawers for bathroom supplies and a range of other accessories.

Flanking maneuvers can help win the battle for storage in a master bedroom. Freestanding units that surround a bed not only contain a useful combination of drawers, shelves, and cabinets, they also add integrated decorating appeal to the room's major piece of furniture. In the examples of closed and open storage illustrated above and at left, one uses a sturdy bridge for display items; the other, a series of shelves and cabinets.

Bedside storage units don't have to be imposingly expensive. In fact, simple solutions are frequently better. Small nightstands that can be bought or built for little money make useful, multipurpose additions to a room, providing space for comfortable access to late-night and early-morning necessities—clocks, radios, books, magazines, newspapers, and more. A piece like the one shown at right is a good example of how a simply built nightstand can be put to work. Large, long shelves yield an abundance of surface area so that books can be placed both vertically and on their sides, ready for the next night's reading. A drop-leaf extension provides space for casual breakfasts in bed. And casters make the unit conveniently mobile.

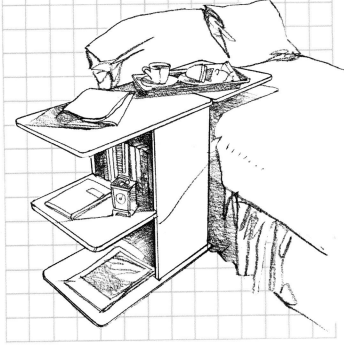

As in other parts of the house, bedroom storage that can hold its own in more ways than one is an invaluable asset. The big unit shown at left is just such a gem. Placed on a pedestal, it's basically a large box (and therefore a project that most do-it-yourselfers can handle). One side serves as a headboard for the bed; on the opposite face is a bank of drawers perfect for folded clothes, blankets, and bed linens. No space is wasted, either: Open bookshelves adorn one end of the box, and display items show off their stuff atop it. Equally important, the entire unit is an effective divider, making the area behind it an excellent spot for a dressing room.

OTHER BEDROOMS

How you arrange storage in your home's other bedrooms depends, to a great extent, on who's using those bedrooms.

Child's play

Children of all ages have known for a long time that a bedroom is much more than a place to sleep the night away. It's an *active* every-minute-of-the-day spot, a room for studying, playing, working on hobbies, and socializing. Where, then, does storage fit into the scheme?

First, kids' rooms should have units that are good-looking and simple to use. Otherwise, many children will tend to store things on the nearest available surface—often the floor. Use your imagination, and decorate cabinets and drawers in eye-catching ways. At the same time, make sure all storage is within easy reach.

In addition, choose pieces that are adaptable enough to keep up with a person who'll not only grow physically, but whose tastes and needs also will change.

To stay flexible, avoid using built-in storage, although units with adjustable shelves and clothes rods can work well. Usually, however, freestanding cabinets, shelves, drawers, and desks are simpler to modify—and add to—as a child matures. Many also make excellent room dividers if two children are sharing the same quarters.

Plan a clothes closet to suit your child's height and reach, changing the position of rods and shelves as necessary. Low, shallow drawers are best for folded clothes; to store shoes, buy or build an expandable rack or set of shelves, and place them beneath hanging clothes.

Toys and games need a place in your scheme, too. For run-of-the-mill items, use storage boxes or bins, maybe with casters to make them mobile. Keep these units low to the ground, so a child can pull out toys and put them away with a minimum of effort. Keep games in or on sliding trays, drawers, or swinging shelves. Display more valuable or attractive objects on open shelving along a wall.

Guest appearances

If you have a bedroom reserved for visitors, storage becomes a different matter entirely.

Start with a bedside unit or units. Stackable modular furniture is often a smart selection because it's so flexible and can fit almost any decorating plan. Other possibilities include bookcases, headboards, and wall-hung shelves.

Drawers are also a necessity. Try to combine drawers and cabinet space into one unit. If floor space is at a premium, tall, thin storage pieces with drawers may do the job and take up less room than ordinary furniture.

As in the master bedroom, under-the-bed storage is a likely alternative. So is an armoire, which can hold everything from clothing and bed linens to books, a TV set, and a stereo system.

Add a writing surface, as well, either a standard table or space-saving options, such as wall-hung units or desks that fold out of bookcases.

The arrangement shown *at right* demonstrates how a child's bedroom can be as much a "living" room as any other part of the house. Many of the storage units also could find a comfortable home in your living room or family room. *(continued)*

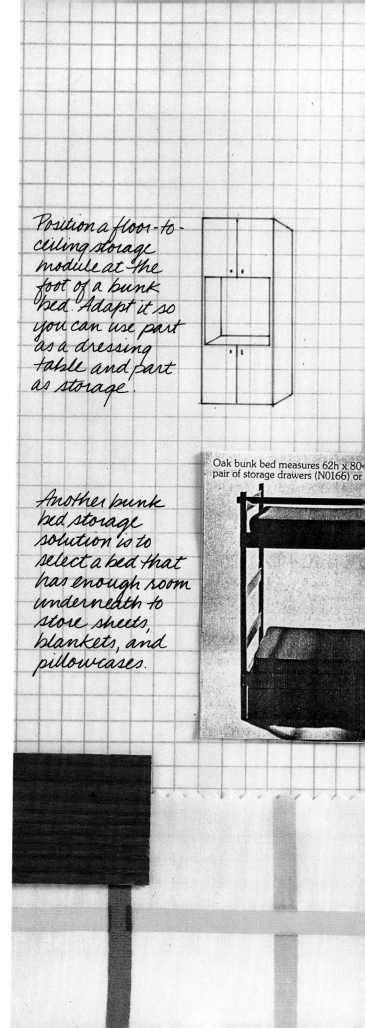

Position a floor-to-ceiling storage module at the foot of a bunk bed. Adapt it so you can use part as a dressing table and part as storage.

Oak bunk bed measures 62h x 80 pair of storage drawers (N0166) or

Another bunk bed storage solution is to select a bed that has enough room underneath to store sheets, blankets, and pillowcases.

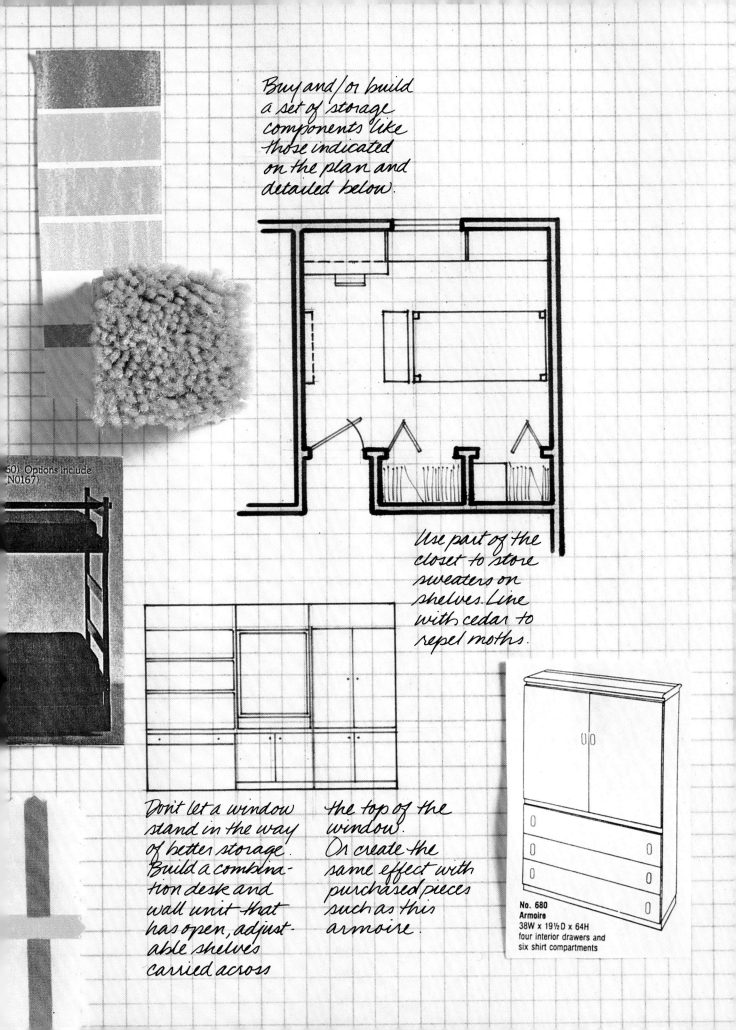

Buy and/or build a set of storage components like those indicated on the plan and detailed below.

Use part of the closet to store sweaters on shelves. Line with cedar to repel moths.

Don't let a window stand in the way of better storage. Build a combination desk and wall unit that has open, adjustable shelves carried across the top of the window. Or create the same effect with purchased pieces such as this armoire.

No. 680
Armoire
38W x 19½D x 64H
four interior drawers and
six shirt compartments

OTHER BEDROOMS

(continued)

When you're planning for kids' rooms, think unconventionally. Children don't need—and aren't likely to want—the same solutions their parents find attractive. For them, storage should be flexible, adaptable, and, above all, colorful. Here are a few build-it-yourself examples.

• You can make an entire wall of storage in a single afternoon by nailing up pine 1x3s to form 2-foot squares. Fill each one with pegboard, cork inserts, display shelves, or blackboards.

• Take old school lockers, such as the ones shown on page 110, and fit them with shelves. Painted with bright, high-gloss colors, they can be just the spot for putting away clothes and toys.

• If two children of different ages are sharing a room, create privacy and storage at the same time by building a free-standing divider with open and closed shelves. Make the enclosed sections openable from either side, with the younger child using the lower shelves; the older child, the upper ones.

Room for one more

Guests—even those who've settled in for more than a day or two—usually don't need an abundance of storage units, just a convenient location to stow a few things temporarily. Generally, one cleared-out closet does nicely for clothes and suitcases, but what if your second bedroom doesn't have one, or its closet is jammed with other possessions?

Simple. Set up a screened partition so it encloses a corner of the room, bring in a clothes rack or install plenty of hooks, and you have a closet. Move in a vanity or bureau, and you have a dressing area.

Devising space-saving, one-of-a-kind storage pieces for a kid's bedroom is a tall order for even the most creative adults. But with a little planning, units such as the one illustrated at left can satisfy many needs and still occupy only a small territory. This project works on a number of levels—a raised bed at the top, wide-open shelves for stashing toys and games below, and large cabinets for hanging clothes and storing shoes, all of which can be stationed in a single corner of the room. Moreover, such a useful furniture combination needn't be forbiddingly drab. Painted with bright designs and matched to the rest of the decor, it can make a kid's room a wonderfully colorful place.

When two kids share a bedroom, squeezing the most out of available space requires imaginative thinking. In the example pictured at right, a large particleboard divider creates privacy for each child, and also serves as a handy, personal bulletin board. But the real stars here are lightweight bunk beds, hinged to the divider, that youngsters can fold up to give themselves more room by attaching a supporting chain to a hook on the partition.

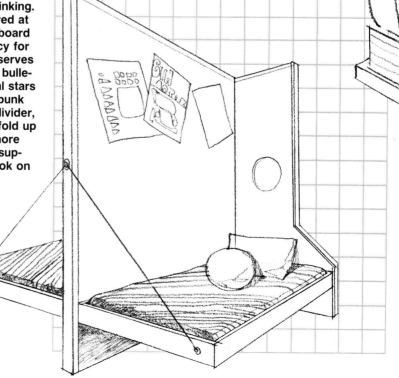

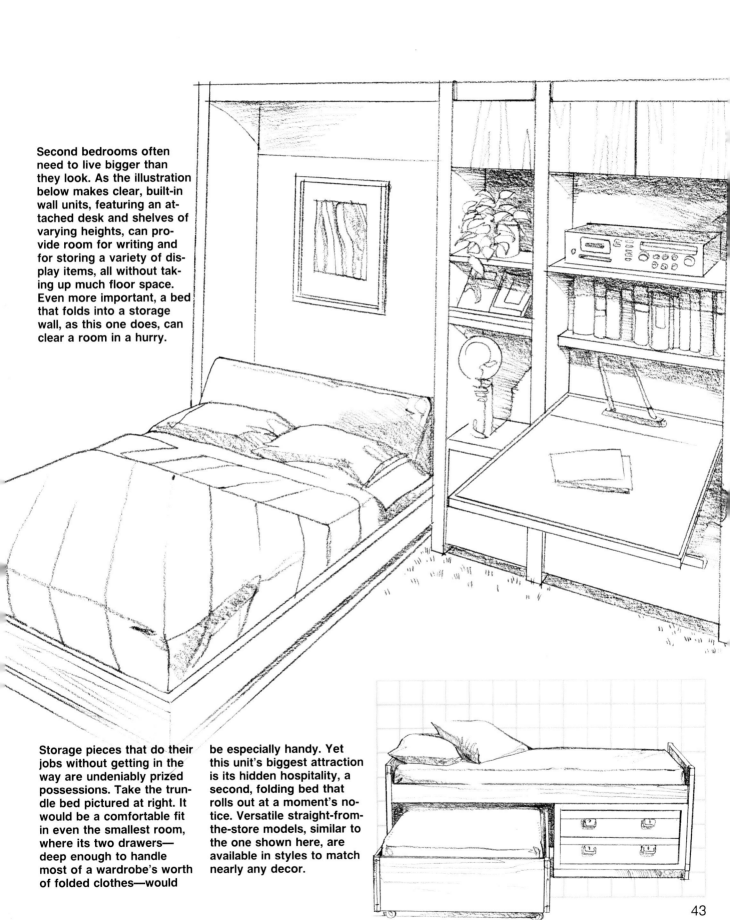

Second bedrooms often need to live bigger than they look. As the illustration below makes clear, built-in wall units, featuring an attached desk and shelves of varying heights, can provide room for writing and for storing a variety of display items, all without taking up much floor space. Even more important, a bed that folds into a storage wall, as this one does, can clear a room in a hurry.

Storage pieces that do their jobs without getting in the way are undeniably prized possessions. Take the trundle bed pictured at right. It would be a comfortable fit in even the smallest room, where its two drawers—deep enough to handle most of a wardrobe's worth of folded clothes—would

be especially handy. Yet this unit's biggest attraction is its hidden hospitality, a second, folding bed that rolls out at a moment's notice. Versatile straight-from-the-store models, similar to the one shown here, are available in styles to match nearly any decor.

43

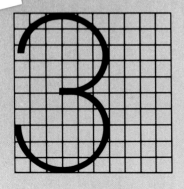

STORAGE BUILDING BASICS

Building simple storage projects is mostly a matter of believing—believing you can do it, even if you're not a whiz with hammer and saw. Once you get the hang of a single fundamental technique—putting together the basic box—you'll know more than enough to create scores of useful things, including the cabinet, closet, bed platform, and storage module described in this chapter.

HOW TO BUILD THE BASIC BOX

Building a box is the first step in putting together a variety of storage units. Bookshelves, cupboards, cabinets, and chests—to name only four common examples—are, essentially, nothing more than simple boxes customized to fit special needs. The boxes shown *at left* will make the various projects described in this chapter. All go together in much the same way.

Sheets of particleboard or plywood are usually the best materials to build with; unlike solid wood they won't lock you into constructing a certain size box. Also, sheet goods' factory-straight edges and large dimensions allow you to make fewer cuts than might otherwise be necessary.

To avoid costly mistakes, sketch a picture of the box, including pertinent measurements, then develop a cutting diagram before you begin to saw. Unless you're using particleboard, plan cuts so the grain of each piece will run in the same direction after the box is assembled. After you're done sawing, make sure all edges are straight and corners square. *(continued)*

HOW TO BUILD
THE BASIC BOX
(continued)

A box isn't a box until you put all the pieces together. To assemble them, try one of three frequently used joinery techniques: the butt joint, miter joint, or rabbet joint.

• *Miter joint*. Using a power saw or a miter box and handsaw (or a backsaw, if you have one), cut the edge of each piece at a 45-degree angle. Then glue and nail together for an attractive fit.

• *Rabbet joint*. This is a particularly sturdy construction technique. To make a rabbet joint, cut away a portion of each edge to be joined so they interlock as shown *opposite, lower right*. Glue and nail.

A table or radial arm saw usually makes the most accurate cuts, but you can also use a portable circular saw, with a 1x3 clamped to the particleboard or plywood. The 1x3 acts as a "rip fence" for the saw.

To construct a butt joint, in which the members meet at a right angle, simply dab glue onto one edge, join, wait a bit, and nail. If you plan to take the box apart later, use screws instead of nails and glue.

The butt joint, bottom, is easy to make and relatively strong. The miter joint, center, is better looking than the other two but also weaker. The rabbet joint, top, is the sturdiest.

47

A CABINET

Nearly every cabinet—from the humblest to the handsomest—is a box with a back, and a door or doors. This 6-foot-tall glass-front display cabinet looks impressive, but it's well within reach of an amateur carpenter. What looks like the most difficult part of the project, building the glass doors, is simply a matter of attaching ready-made glazed units to the oak box.

Although oak lumber is certainly more expensive than either particleboard or plywood, assembling a cabinet like this on your own will be much less costly than buying a comparable unit at a furniture outlet. And, without a doubt, it's an impressive piece of work that can stand up to all but the very best ready-made models.

To begin, have the lumberyard cut 1x12s to your specifications (the cabinet shown *opposite* is 6 feet high, but you can vary the dimensions as you wish). Then, build a basic box, mitering the corners at top and bottom.

The back is a ⅛-inch-thick clear acrylic sheet. Buy the material cut to size. Then, using a router, rabbet the box's back edges and attach the sheet, drilling and screwing it in place, as shown in the photograph *at upper right*.

The doors for this project are 12x72-inch stock glazed sidelights, available at building supply stores. Attach each with three brass hinges, located near the top, bottom, and middle of the unit. Then, install magnetic catches along the top and bottom, and add knobs to the doors (the ones shown here are porcelain).

Fit the cabinet with adjustable oak plywood shelves, and finish everything by applying clear satin varnish.

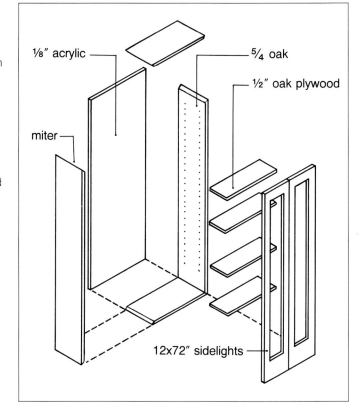

⅛" acrylic

5/4 oak

½" oak plywood

miter

12x72" sidelights

A CLOSET

Gaining more closet space needn't involve building-in. You can construct a spacious new closet without making any changes in your walls. Building a free-standing closet like the one shown on the opposite page puts extra storage where you need it most. The deep, hinged door rolls out to provide even more space for keeping things.

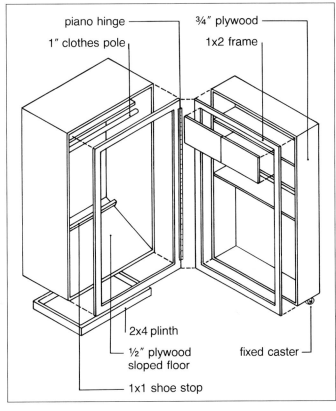

piano hinge

1" clothes pole

¾" plywood

1x2 frame

2x4 plinth

½" plywood
sloped floor

1x1 shoe stop

fixed caster

First, put together the stationary part, using ¾-inch fir plywood for the back, sides, top, and bottom. The closet shown here is 3½ feet wide, 2 feet deep, and 70 inches high.

Then, build the hinged door, also from ¾-inch plywood. Make it 10 inches deep, and match the other dimensions described above (or comparable ones you've chosen to work with).

Line each section with cedar (you might be able to pick up precut pieces at a lumber-yard). Nail the wood in place. As you proceed, butt the joints, and cut the wood to the proper length.

Next, install ¾-inch plywood shelves and the clothes pole, centering the pole a foot or so from the top. To build the shoe rack, nail angled 1x2s to the sides and fit the shelf. It will need miter cuts top and bottom. A 1x1-inch strip nailed to the shelf serves as a hook for heels. Then, nail a 1x2 surround frame to the front edges of each box, and hang the two small doors.

To build a base for the stationary section, use 2x4s on edge, recessing them about 2 inches from each end of the closet. Attach a heavy-duty caster—the same height as the base—to the door.

To join both parts, screw a full-length piano hinge to the larger section's 1x2 frame, as shown in the photograph *at upper left*, then attach the other hinge leaf to the smaller section.

This closet has been outfitted for storing clothing, but you can customize the unit to hold other items. Turn to page 143 to see a similar closet outfitted to store linens and bathroom supplies.

STORAGE BUILDING BASICS

A BED PLATFORM

A simple mattress platform with a roll-out bin beneath provides lots of storage in the same floor space that the bed occupies. Surround the bed with more customized storage at the head, foot, and sides to put books, radio, alarm clock, and more within arm's reach. This is obviously a child's room, but a similar platform storage system would work just as well for a sleeper of any age. The footboard, side units, and movable storage underneath are an assembly of different-size boxes.

In one productive afternoon, you can build the bed platform shown *at right,* as well as the headboard (not shown), footboard, side units, and storage area underneath—all using the basic techniques described in this chapter.

As with other projects, first make a sketch to the dimensions you need. How large you build each box will depend on the size of the mattress and objects to be stored. The headboard and footboard, for example, can be widened or narrowed, as necessary, and the side units can be deepened. Instead of leaving it completely open, you can enclose the side storage, add shelves to it, or both. This bed platform, built to accept a twin-size mattress, is 75 inches long, 39 inches wide, and 4 inches high.

Once you have the measurements in order, begin building. Which box you start with makes no difference. Use particleboard, cut the pieces to size, and assemble each component with flathead wood screws, butt-joining the edges.

Then screw the platform to the headboard, footboard, and side unit. You might choose to make front edges flush, as shown in the inset photo, or recess them slightly. Finish all surfaces with paint or plastic laminate.

Add casters to the bottom storage box. Plastic wheels work best on soft surfaces; rubber wheels on concrete, vinyl, or hardwood. Recess the casters enough to hide them from view when the storage unit is closed.

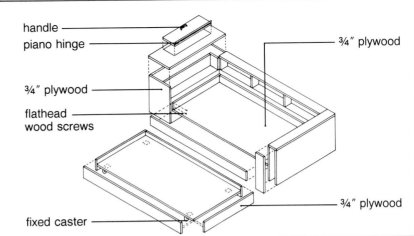

handle

piano hinge

¾" plywood

¾" plywood

flathead
wood screws

fixed caster

¾" plywood

¾" plywood

A STORAGE MODULE

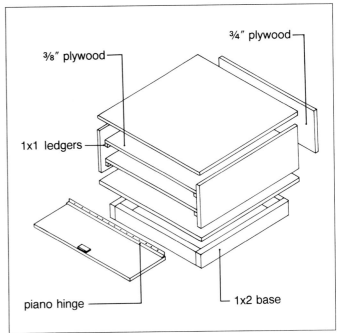

¾" plywood

⅜" plywood

1x1 ledgers

piano hinge

1x2 base

There's nothing mysterious about *this* black box. Made from plywood and rubber floor tiles, it's a hardworking coffee table and handy storage system all built into one versatile piece of furniture. Comfortable enough to rest an elbow on, it's a perfect hideaway for large posters, paintings, jigsaw puzzles, or sheets of paper you can't easily stash elsewhere.

This large storage module sits atop a smaller four-sided frame, or plinth, that's inset 3 inches on every side. Build the main compartment in any dimensions you choose, then size the support plinth accordingly.

Make the bigger box—top, sides, ends, and bottom—using ¾-inch plywood. Build the plinth from 1x2s, as shown in the drawing *top, right*.

As pictured in the photograph *top, left*, glue and nail 1x1 stops, or ledger strips, to the sides of the storage box. The shelves will rest loosely on top of the strips and should slide in and out easily. (To show how the whole unit fits together, the photo shows the ledgers being nailed into the finished box. You'll find it easier to attach the ledgers *before* you assemble the box.)

To complete the main compartment and plinth, butt-join all edges, gluing and nailing them together. Use flathead wood screws to attach the larger unit to the frame.

Then, install a piano hinge for the drop-down door, and add a magnetic, collar, or friction catch to keep it in place.

Next, cut the shelves to fit, using ⅜- or ¾-inch plywood. Make sure to allow a ⅛-inch clearance all the way around.

The rubber surface, often used as commercial flooring, is a tough but attractive material. Simply cut it to size, and apply with mastic, slightly mitering at corners for a snug, neat fit.

One of the nice things about making this unit is that it doesn't box you in to a single set of building instructions. For example, instead of using flooring, you can either paint or stain the boxes and shelves or apply some other kind of dura-ble surface material to them. If you plan to leave the wood exposed, you may prefer to miter joints for a neater appearance.

At the same time, you don't have to use 1x1 ledgers as support for the shelves. Screwing in extendible hardware, which you can buy at any building supply store, is an equally effective option. It's a little more costly and time-consuming to install (you have to make sure the hardware is perfectly level), but it does prevent the shelves from tipping, something they occasionally might do if you use ledger strips alone.

Finally, you may discover a need for even more storage space later on. No problem. Just build another box or boxes of the same size, and either stack them together or set them side by side.

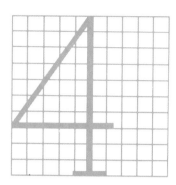

ALL ABOUT SHELVES

Shelves. Every home has them, yet everyone in the family always seems to want more and more—room to store a great, ever-expanding collection of books, albums, pictures, trophies, magazines, clothing, and the multitude of other things all houses are heir to. This chapter explains how to use shelves, how to build them, and how to buy them.

Compared to fancy cabinets and opulent dressers, shelves often are at the bottom of the wish list when it comes to making or buying storage units. They're useful, and you wouldn't want to do without them, but when you think of shelves you may be thinking only of the battered metal models crowding countless garages.

If shelving ever was limited to those metal units, it isn't any more. All shelves have horizontal surfaces and some are indeed made of metal, but they come in many styles, sizes, and materials.

You can find hanging shelves, sliding shelves, revolving shelves, and shelves that pop up or drop down. Also available are built-in shelves, cantilevered shelves, and shelves that stand on their own. You can put together simple units in a matter of minutes using concrete blocks and a few spare pieces of lumber. Or you can buy or build eye-opening decorative models made of wood, metal, or plastic.

Whatever the type, however, every horizontal shelfpiece needs three things: solid vertical support, stable connections where it joins an upright, and enough strength to bear the weight of all objects meant to be placed atop it.

The shelving that's best for you, then, depends to a great extent on what you plan to store. It also depends on how accessible you want the items to be, where you want to put them, and how well the shelving itself blends with the rest of a room's decorating scheme.

Room service
Just as you wouldn't think of storing paint cans or spare tires in the bedroom, neither would you want the kinds of storage appropriate for those objects playing a leading role in one of your home's living areas. The following is a point-by-point rundown of shelving ideas.

• *Living centers*. Family rooms, living rooms, dining rooms, and bedrooms all have lots of wall space that you can take advantage of with a single large unit or a series of smaller ones. The unit shown *opposite*, for example, houses books, records, a stereo, and a television in a sleek, contemporary setting—and features a closed section that drops down to serve as a game table.

Shelving placed in highly visible locations like these should be good-looking, carefully finished, and thoughtfully tailored to the room's furniture and color patterns. The design of a unit must suit the items you plan to store. Conventional bookcases, for instance, are no more than basic boxes of varying dimensions. Where you install the horizontal pieces that transform the boxes into bookshelves depends on the size of the volumes you'll put on display. The same advice applies to traditional shelves of any kind, whether they hang from a wall, rise from floor to ceiling, sit atop a cabinet, or are partially built-in.

For smaller objects you'd prefer to keep in a certain part of the house but out of view when they're not in use—toys and games, for example—special shelving can provide all the storage you need. Folding units, with one section anchored to a wall and additional swinging compartments supported by casters, will yield a great deal of storage without consuming valuable floor space. *(continued)*

SHELVING ALTERNATIVES
(continued)

For specific uses, shelves can be notched, slotted, or drilled full of holes to serve as resting places for everything from hats to fine glassware.

When you need attractive, simple shelf space fast, think of constructing easy-to-assemble unfinished wood units, like the freestanding version shown *opposite*. They'll quickly clear a cluttered bedroom or playroom floor. Moreover, you can take apart this kind of shelving in a flash and reassemble the parts wherever you need a fast solution to a storage problem.

• *Kitchens*. Built-in cabinets are most people's choice, but shelves of various kinds also can be big helps in the kitchen. In fact, one way to improve the basic cabinet is to divide it into shelves designed to hold individual items, such as pots, pans, and baking tins.

Like those in other parts of the house, kitchen shelves can be notched, slotted, or cut to hold specific objects. And you can hide floor-to-ceiling models behind entranceways and even add one or more units to the doors themselves.

The deep, built-in shelves in the photograph *at right* are pretty and highly effective. Each piece of china and stoneware is not only within easy reach, it is also part of a handsome display. (For more about versatile kitchen storage, see Chapter 5.)

• *Bathrooms*. Just finding a place for storage can be a problem here. Small wall-hung units are often the most utilitarian solution. You also may be able to build shelving next to and around a toilet or sink. (For more about bathroom storage, see Chapter 6.)

SHELVES
YOU CAN
BUILD

Once you've decided where you're going to put the shelves and what you're going to store on them, you may want to try your hand at assembling hardworking units similar to the ones shown here. All are made of 1-inch pine, and three are little more than easy-to-build basic boxes (see Chapter 3—"Storage Building Basics").

Two have ⅛-inch tempered hardboard backs, but other materials would serve equally well. For the shelves themselves, you also might use plywood or another type of lumber. Avoid using hardboard and particleboard for shelves; they bow under heavy loads.

Pertinent dimensions
Like what you see? Here are the vital statistics for shelves shown on these pages.

5

2

4

1

This simple pair of long boxes (1) is 6½ feet high by 14 inches wide by 11½ inches deep. Several placed on end can provide a whole wall of storage. Here, the verticals, as well as the shelves, were cut from 1x12s and backed by ¼-inch plywood.

Make this unit (2) using 1x3s for the vertical members, 1x1s for the vertical shelf supports, and 1x12s for the shelves.

These two butt-joined boxes (3) measure 36x12x11½ inches deep. Construct as many as you need, and stack them.

To put together this small two-shelf unit (4), notch 1x12s to receive 1x2s with 1x8 shelves nailed between them.

This is another basic box (5)—60x30x11½ inches deep. Adjustable clips support each of the unit's shelves.

Means of support

For any project made of wood, you can choose one of several ways to mount the horizontal shelfpieces.

Inexpensive *clips* are easy to install and allow you to change the position of individual horizontal members. Using *dowels* is another way to make movable shelves. In the sides of the uprights drill several holes equal to the diameter of the dowels (¼ inch for light loads, ⅜ inch for heavier weights), boring them deep enough to accept at least ½ inch of the dowels' length. Use a level to make sure the holes align with each other.

One way to set shelves in a fixed position is to *butt-join* them to vertical members with nails and screws. Use this method, however, only to support light or moderate loads, and not for plywood shelves.

Screwing in small shelf supports, or *cleats,* made of solid wood or particleboard and about the same thickness as the shelf itself is a second effective technique. *Dadoing* the uprights to receive each shelf is a third alternative (for more about support systems, see pages 68 and 69).

3

PLANNING A SHELVING SYSTEM

Good-looking, hardworking shelving starts with a carefully worked-out plan. Not only does a plan help you visualize the results, it also enables you to develop an accurate materials list, which can spare you a second trip to the lumberyard or a pile of expensive leftovers.

Any shelves must fit the space available. First, precisely measure the height, depth, and width of the walls that will surround the unit. Take special note of any structural features, such as pipes and baseboards, that you'll have to work around.

Then, from these dimensions, subtract the thicknesses of the materials you'll use for the sides, back and front, and top and bottom. The results represent the amount of space you'll be able to use.

Now decide what you want to store, gauging each object's height, width, and depth. If you plan to put away items of greatly varying sizes or stack smaller ones together, measure the largest and smallest in the group (consider each stack a single item). With these dimensions in mind, you can determine the most economical shelf spacing.

This also is the time to consider different configurations. For example, you might want shelves of various widths and depths in the same unit. Or, you may prefer to make the shelving partially or completely closed.

The shelving systems shown in the photographs *at right* (and the larger ones on the next four pages) are two equally acceptable ways to build into the space occupied by the furniture piece in the picture *at left*. For more about these built-in shelving units, see the pages that follow.

The shelves of this attractive unit are wide and deep enough to handle an entire set of tableware, and the doors protect against dust.

The open shelving pictured here shows off collectibles to great effect. Different shelf spacing makes it a versatile storage place.

SHELVING SPANS

The longer a shelf, the more support it needs. Assuming a full, heavy load, here are the maximum safe distances between supports:

¾-inch plywood	36″
1x12 lumber	24″
2x10 or 2x12 lumber	48-56″
½-inch acrylic	22″
½-inch glass	18″

BUILDING A SHELVING SYSTEM

Building a picture-perfect shelf unit like the one in the photograph *at left* or the open system shown on the next two pages is not a snap, but even a very complicated shelving project can be pulled off by a reasonably experienced do-it-yourselfer. When you're tackling complex assignments, keep the following general steps in mind.

• Incorporating the dimensions you calculated earlier, sketch a design of the whole project on a piece of paper before you begin building. This needn't be a finished drawing done to scale, but, for most shelving units, the measurements must be *absolutely* accurate.

• Compile a list of materials, buy those you don't already have on hand, and make sure you have the appropriate tools to work with.

• Transfer measurements to the wood, and cut carefully. Again, accuracy is critically important.

• Next, cut all joints, then glue and nail (or screw) the main pieces together. Butt, dado, and rabbet joints are the most common ways to assemble shelving units. Using one of these standard joints, attach the horizontal shelfpieces themselves to the uprights, or install a separate hardware support system (see pages 68 and 69).

• With the principal unit constructed, buy or build and then install any secondary parts, or subassemblies, that are part of the project. For the system pictured here, the bottom of the unit and the doors (purchased from a lumberyard) are subassemblies, with the bottom attached directly to the wall and the doors added later to finish the job. *(continued)*

A rough drawing of the unit is a key first step in the building process. Indicate exact spacing for each shelf support.

In this shelving system, a front piece and ledger strips attached to the wall support the bottom securely, yet unobtrusively.

Loose-pin hinges secured to premade doors and attached to the stiles help to close off and protect everything stored on the shelves.

65

BUILDING A SHELVING SYSTEM

(continued)

Most shelving projects made of wood aren't finished until they're finished, and some protective coatings require more work than others. Units you plan to keep out of sight—in a basement, attic, or garage, for example—don't need much at all. Just sand them lightly and apply a clear sealer to protect the wood from dirt and grime.

On the other hand, decorative shelves for your home's living areas often demand special treatment, depending, in part, on what you want to store and how you want the unit to look in relation to the rest of the room. In many cases, paint is a serviceable, colorful option. Alkyd enamels are usually the best choice for shelves, but urethane paints also are good, because they stand up so well to wear and tear. Epoxy paints provide an equally tough finish, but they're tricky to apply. Ordinary latex paints may be all right for shelves that won't get much abuse. Otherwise, avoid using them: They don't wear well.

You also might consider alternatives to standard paint. So-called antiquing paints are a satisfactory middle ground between regular paints and stains. They produce a darker finish that blends attractively into more subdued room designs. For clear and natural-stain finishes, use shellac, varnish, polyurethane varnish, or penetrating resins.

High-gloss finishes are very tough and easy to keep clean, although they reflect a lot of light. Semigloss and satin finishes may be more eye-pleasing selections.

Whatever your choice, don't skimp on preparation. Shelves must be sanded and filled properly before you can finish the work.

Like the one shown at left, shelving systems that hold collectibles must have stanchions (vertical supports) that are perfectly plumb.

Shelves should be level, sturdy, and tip-free. Here, small but sturdy shelf clips securely support shelf ends.

SHELVING
HARDWARE AND
SUPPORT SYSTEMS

2

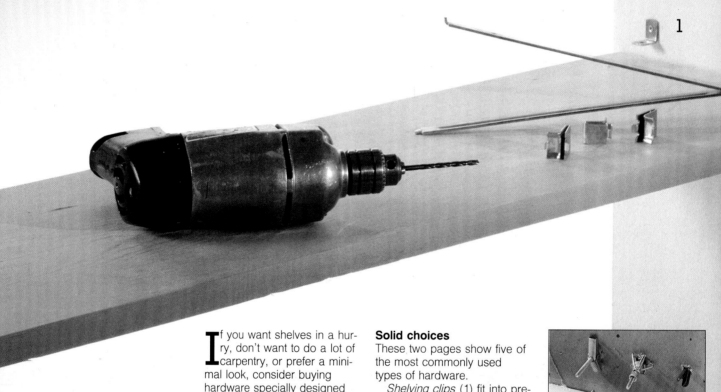

1

If you want shelves in a hurry, don't want to do a lot of carpentry, or prefer a minimal look, consider buying hardware specially designed for shelving projects. Hardware systems vary. Here's how to choose the one that will play the best supporting role for your shelves.

First, some questions. How much weight must the hardware support, and how long are the shelving spans (see page 63)? Will the shelves mount at the rear, or at the ends? Should brackets be fixed or adjustable? Is hardware even necessary? Maybe wooden cleats or dado joints would work better.

Appearance is important as well. Hardware styles range from small clips to angled brackets that support magazine racks. As styles differ, so do prices. Some hardware may be more expensive than the shelving itself.

Solid choices

These two pages show five of the most commonly used types of hardware.

Shelving clips (1) fit into pre-drilled holes. Inexpensive, they can support heavy loads on ¾-inch-thick boards with spans of up to 30 inches.

Clips and *strips* (2) allow you to adjust end-mounted shelves (again, an acceptable maximum span is 30 inches). If possible, dado the sides of the bookcase so you can recess the strips flush with the surface.

Decorative brackets (3) come in many sizes, shapes, and finishes. They're often *not* adjustable.

Knife brackets and *strips* (4) are adjustable and can hold their own with any support system. Select 8-, 10-, or 12-inch brackets.

Angle brackets (5) bear medium-weight loads. Mount them with their longer legs against the wall.

The best fasteners for most hardware systems are wood screws drilled straight into a stud. This method, however, limits where you can place the shelves. The hollow-wall fasteners shown in the small photograph *above*—from left to right, toggle bolt, expansion bolt, and plastic anchor—are three trustworthy alternatives. Be sure to use plastic anchors, however, only to support relatively light loads.

3

4

5

SHELVES
TO BUY

If time is of the essence, or you really don't like to build things, why not just buy ready-made units? You may end up spending only slightly more money for simple ready-mades than you'd pay for the materials you'd need to build similar shelving.

As this photograph indicates, shelves are many-splendored things. You'll find them made of finished and unfinished wood, metal, coated metal wire, acrylic, and several different kinds of plastic. Some are freestanding units; others are wall-hung models. Many are entirely open; some are partially or completely closed. Certain kinds are designed specifically to store record albums, books, and other household items.

You'll discover adjustable shelving, knock-down shelving, even shelving that can do double duty (like the unit with a desk shown here). By shopping at department stores, lumberyards, do-it-yourself centers, and office supply outlets, you'll be able to find units sized and shaped to fit your space, needs, and budget.

Old reliables

Two types of shelving often provide the most storage for the least money.

• *Unfinished bookcases,* which you can cover any way you like, are available in many modular sizes. Line them up or stack them wherever you need open shelving. The best models feature rabbeted backs and dadoed shelves, with surfaces that require only light sanding.

• *Open-frame steel* units have shelves as deep as 24 inches, stand on their own, and work equally well against a wall or as room dividers. Buy only models with strong posts and sturdy locking systems.

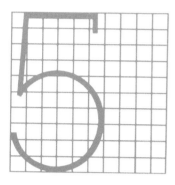

KITCHEN STORAGE

What you store and how you store it determine how well you and your kitchen work together. Whether you frequently use complex gadgets or visit the kitchen only once a day, where you keep utensils and ingredients is almost as important as having the right materials to start with. In this chapter, we show you examples of good kitchen storage, some of it basic, some of it highly imaginative. We hope you find it a useful lesson in kitchen compatibility.

PLANNING KITCHEN STORAGE

The size and shape of your kitchen and the amount and kind of cooking you do should influence the way you plan storage. How—and how much—you entertain, how often you shop for groceries, how many people you have in your family, and how many of them cook also affect your planning.

One general rule holds true for just about any combination of situations, however: *Store items as close as possible to where you use them.*

In most kitchens, the place to start planning storage is at the three basic work centers—food preparation, cooking, and cleanup. Each center has its own functions and its own specific storage needs.

Cabinets between two work centers may share duties, storing items for both centers. A few items, such as measuring spoons, often may be used at two locations. Rather than decide on one spot for them, consider buying duplicates. Generally, however, kitchen tools and ingredients have one center where they're most at home and most needed.

Food preparation
The food preparation center must accommodate grocery storage—perishables, staples, and specialty items such as spices. How much food storage you need depends on the size of your family and on your shopping patterns.

The food preparation center is also where you should keep the utensils needed for making salads, grinding and shredding foods, preparing main dishes, packing lunches, and mixing batters.

In addition to food, some of the items it makes sense to store near this center include appliances such as blenders, mixers, and food processors;

baking equipment such as cookie sheets, measuring cups and spoons, mixing bowls and spoons, and baking tins; salad-making needs such as cutting boards, salad bowls, colanders, and knives; and assorted other food preparation items such as casseroles, molds, and refrigerator-freezer and other storage containers.

Cooking
Near the range and oven you'll want space for cookware and cooking utensils, serving bowls and platters, and counter-top cooking appliances such as electric skillets, griddles, and slow cookers.

Cleanup
In addition to storing cleaning supplies and a wastebasket or trash container, the area near the sink and dishwasher is a handy place for any other item whose use primarily involves water—saucepans, coffee makers, and double boilers, for example. Also make room here for a vegetable brush and peeler, strainer, and frequently used dishes, flatware, and glasses.

Organized storage
Successful storage means having the things you use most often closest at hand. Here are some guidelines for planning efficient storage:
• Sort through kitchen items periodically. If you use an item only once or twice a year, find a place for it out of the kitchen.
• Reserve space at the front of shelves and cabinets for items you use often.
• For convenient access, store frequently used items no lower than 22 inches and no higher than 72 inches from the floor.
• For cookware and utensils in use daily, try open-shelf, hanging, or counter-top storage.

COOKWARE

Good cooks attribute their success to a variety of things—special techniques, exotic spices, secret recipes. Another essential ingredient is the right utensil, right at hand—not buried in a drawer or cabinet on the other side of the room. Here are some suggestions for well-organized, safe, and close-at-hand storage.

Does the utensil-storage squeeze have you climbing the walls? That may not be so bad: Walls offer a surprisingly large amount of storage space.

In the kitchen shown *above*, niches in the wall next to and above the ovens, plus a metal rail *above* the cooktop, put spatulas, spoons, serving trays, and spices where they're needed most.

Walls also live up to their storage potential when you use them to anchor perforated hardboard or plastic-coated wire grids and baskets. The latter are available in a variety of colors, shapes, and sizes. Both hardboard and wire systems are easy to mount, and store everything from cookware to stirring tools.

Another way walls can help expand storage space is by

housing your oven—conventional, microwave, or convection. If you're doing any kitchen remodeling, consider installing a counter-top cook surface and a wall oven to free space for cabinet storage.

The kitchen shown *above* is a high-style illustration of this technique. Three sleek drawers beneath the cooktop store equipment just inches from where it's needed.

A counter-top cache is perfect for storing small, basic utensils. *At right,* a stainless steel box 6 inches deep has been set into a recess at the back edge of the counter. The recessed space measures about 4 inches from counter to wall.

Commercial flatware storage units, available in restaurant supply stores and some housewares shops, can be recessed behind a new counter top or placed on top of an existing one. Look for stainless steel flatware baskets or cylindrical plastic containers.

Counter-top storage doesn't have to stop at the back of the counter. Use anything from a stainless steel mesh test-tube basket to a rugged stoneware crock wherever you need utensils within easy reach. Just be sure that any container you use is heavy or broad-based so it won't tip or slide.

S uspended storage makes sense wherever surface space is at a premium. Here's a revised version of the familiar ceiling-hung pot racks of classic country kitchens.

Two pine brackets support a metal grid equipped with hangers and topped by a glass shelf. Any utensil with a pierced or ringed handle will find a place to hang here. Better yet, the unit really has two levels of storage—one for hangables below and one for lightweight baskets and baking pans above.

The result is not just efficient, convenient-yet-out-of-the-way storage, but also a pleasing blend of natural wood's warmth and high-tech geometry.

COOKWARE
(continued)

Make drawer space more efficient with dividers. Instead of a clanging pile of pans, trays, and lids, you can have neatly sorted sections for each item or group of items.

Dividers can be engineered in several ways and spaced irregularly to allow for oddly shaped items. *Below,* vertical hardboard dividers are held in place by U-shaped plastic clips that press like thumbtacks into the front and back walls of the drawer. Note that this bakeware drawer is sensibly located below the oven.

Get a similar effect by attaching slotted boards to the front and back of the drawer unit, then slipping hardboard dividers into the slots. Move dividers as your needs change.

In small or unusually proportioned drawers, think of modular plastic storage units. They're widely available, easy to use, inexpensive, and versatile. They come in many configurations, so you can arrange them to suit almost any space.

The slide-out appliance center *above* is a drawer with a difference. The front drops down to become a working shelf, and the back of the drawer is fitted with electrical outlets so that appliances stored in the drawer can be used in place. Here, a lack of dividers gives flexibility to the storage space and allows easier mobility for the appliances; for prolonged use they're moved to more accessible counter height. The drawer's laminate-clad interior is a breeze to clean.

If you'd like to install a similar drawer in your kitchen, plan approximately half the space between counter top and floor for the depth of the drawer. This allows room for larger appliances such as food processors or blenders.

Islands are most often created to supplement countertop work surfaces, but underneath their smooth top layers is valuable storage space. The two photos on this page feature two islands designed for specialized storage in one large, carefully remodeled kitchen.

Shown *at right* is a handy food preparation/entertainment center equipped with bar sink, butcher block top, and pop-up cookbook holder. Below the work surface, a cabinet shelters cookware and mixers. The top shelf lifts to extend the counter top, letting the cook use the large mixer without moving it. Under the lift-up unit, an adjustable shelf divides the remaining space into a pair of parking places for small appliances and shallow bakeware.

The pop-up principle is at work in the photo *at left,* too. Here, the food processor is stored on a lift-up shelf similar to the one that houses the mixer. Additional drawers beside this cabinet store the processor's blades.

If you're designing custom cabinets and want to include lift-up shelves, here are some things to keep in mind.
• Decide what you'll be storing and make sure to provide enough clearance space for the unit to function when the stored items are in place.
• Plan easy-to-clean surfaces for any shelf that will serve as an extension of your countertop work space.
• Provide power outlets in or near cabinets that will store portable appliances. Otherwise you'll defeat the purpose of having the lift-up units in the first place.

TABLEWARE

Dishes, glasses, and flatware are the bread-and-butter utensils of any kitchen. They move in and out of storage more often than any other items, and they're likely to be missed more than just about anything else when you can't find the right ones. Here are three sparkling storage ideas to make tableware easier to find and faster to put away.

If you're proud of your dishes and think they're worth putting on display, open shelving like that shown *opposite* is a convenient storage arrangement well worth considering. Whether you choose open or closed shelving for your kitchen, here are some sizes to keep in mind.

• A 12-inch-deep shelf accommodates most dishes except serving platters. Plate storage deeper than 12 inches requires reaching over one set of items to get to another; the layered look is far from ideal for storage convenience.

• Shelves for glassware and cups or mugs should be 4 to 6 inches deep—no more, for the same reason explained above.

The two shelves pictured *at right* borrow from the way dishwashers are organized to provide efficient storage for mealtime equipment.

The two shelves are fitted with plastic-coated wire racks that make vertical storage of dishes easy and keep breakable items from crashing into one another. Cups and bowls are assigned spaces next to the dish racks.

A compact unit like this is easy to make out of an existing cabinet or pair of drawers. This one is located next to the dishwasher to save time and energy in putting away clean dishes.

Tableware shelves needn't be in one large, built-in unit—or even in the kitchen. The compartments shown *above,* for example, make super-efficient use of the bottom space in a sleekly laminated dining room buffet.

Lined up along the base are several clearly defined storage units. A dish drawer equipped with separators keeps dishes upright; a pair of sliding shelves, camouflaged by fold-down doors, keeps cups, saucers, and bowls in order. At the end of the buffet, table linens tuck tidily away on narrow slide-out shelves.

This kind of everything-in-its-place storage isn't limited to any one style of furniture. Contemporary storage units look so efficient and clean-lined that they make you want to be organized too—but space is space, no matter what it looks like on the outside. For example, a turn-of-the-century sideboard with a multitude of drawers is just as ready-made for compartmentalized storage as the smoothest, sleekest modular unit.

PANTRY IDEAS

No self-respecting turn-of-the-century home was without a spacious pantry, a room just off the kitchen that had shelves laden with staples and home-canned fruits and vegetables. Now the pantry is back, albeit in modified form. It may be a large cabinet within the kitchen, and it may store as much convenience food as home-grown produce, but the concept is the same: efficient food storage in one accessible location.

Kitchen closets make great pantries when they're designed to make use of every bit of space. The closet shown *below,* for example, has been fitted with U-shaped shelves just deep enough so that all the items stored on them are visible. A second shelf, built on the inside of the closet door, fits into the recess created by the U. The result is as much storage space as standard-depth shelves, but a lot more visibility and accessibility.

In a pantry of any size, plan for shallow shelves. Optimum shelf width is the depth of two cans or jars. With a larger pantry area, you will find it easier to keep track of things if you break up the area into smaller spaces. Dividers, racks, and trays can all help you organize.

For example, the generously dimensioned custom-built pantry pictured *opposite* stores more than food. Horizontally divided space houses place mats, a roll-out work/storage unit, even a fruit and herb drier. The main feature, however, is row after row of shallow, U-shaped shelves lining the top portion of the walls. Larger shelves below the counter store items bought in bulk. Keep in mind that storing foods of the same type together makes it easier for you to take inventory at a glance.

Pantry placement
The ideal location for a pantry is in or near the kitchen, but environmental conditions also are important, and you should consider them before determining where to put your pantry. Among the points to consider are these:
• Pantries should be dry. Many types of food, especially staples such as sugar, flour, pasta, crackers, and other loose, dry foods, are adversely affected by high humidity.
• Pantries should be cool. Many foods deteriorate faster in warmer temperatures. Avoid placing a pantry near sources of heat, including ranges, ovens, and radiators.
• Pantries should be dark. Some foods, especially those stored in glass containers, may be damaged by light. If your pantry has a window, include a room-darkening window covering in your plans.

PANTRY IDEAS
(continued)

If you don't have an ideal kitchen closet or corner just waiting to be converted to a pantry, the next best location may be just around the corner, in a corridor, hallway, or entry adjacent to the kitchen.

A pantry located in a hallway near the kitchen has several advantages. Chances are it's close to the door you use to bring groceries into the house. The climate is likely to be comfortably cool, because a hallway usually has no heating outlet—and no window to let in light and heat from the sun.

When you plan a hallway pantry, keep these special considerations in mind.
• Make sure your food storage area doesn't interfere with hallway traffic—or vice versa.
• Use space all the way to the ceiling; handy, long-handled grabbers make it possible to reach top-shelf storage without a step stool.

Contemporary versus country

The double-deck pantry shown *opposite* is set up in a kitchen corridor. Plastic laminate sheathes the shelves and doors for easy maintenance and a sleek look. The adjustable shelves are supported by metal standards and brackets.

The equally serviceable hallway pantry pictured *at right* is a re-creation of the old pierced-tin pie case. Patterned tin ceiling material, framed by mellow pine, creates an old-time pantry with lots of room for up-to-the-minute ingredients and equipment.

SPICES
AND
STAPLES

Little things can create a lot of storage problems in a kitchen. So can sacks of flour, economy-size boxes of cereal, and bulky, loose produce. Organization is the key here. If you plan right, everything will be just where it should be, neatly arranged, not hidden by a neighboring item and not blocking access to whatever it is you really want. With a little storage planning, you can have the rosemary, sage, basil, and powdered mustard right where you want them, never run out of your children's favorite cereal on a busy morning, and know right away whether you can make baked potatoes for dinner without a special trip to the market.

A cabinet outside a cabinet is one solution to the problem of spices that go astray on a large shelf. As shown *above*, spices are neatly lined up on seven shelves of a shallow exterior cabinet, hinged so it can serve as the door to a standard corner cabinet. It's a space-efficient variation of the familiar wall-hung wooden spice rack.

A glass front keeps the spice jars free of dust but easy to see. The solid backing on the inner side of the spice rack conceals dishes and glassware, and keeps the jars from sliding backward when the door is opened or closed.

The drawer *opposite* keeps spices out of the way but within reach. It is equipped with angled dividers supported by wooden wedges. Spice jars lean back on the wedges, and the bottoms of the jars in one row rest on the divider of the row ahead.

This is a simple do-it-yourself project. Once you decide how many dividers you need, glue the wedges to the drawer and slip the dividers into place.

The kitchen *above* combines clean-lined surfaces and efficient layout with the old-time charm of country store storage bins. Each tilt-out bin houses one variety of bulky produce and would be equally suitable for flour, sugar, rice, crackers, or other dry staples.

These bins are made of ¾-inch plywood and framed in ¾-inch solid oak to match the trim on appliances and

counters. The windows are made of tempered plate glass; transparent acrylic is a safe alternative. The important thing is to avoid fragile standard window glass, which could shatter into the food.

Examine the drawing *at right* and you can see how the bins pivot outward for access. Lift straight up on a bin and you can remove it for thorough, easy cleaning.

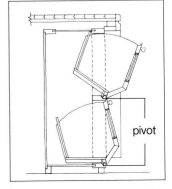

pivot

OUTFITTING CABINETS

If nothing has a place in your kitchen, or too many kitchen items are in the same place, the problem may not be a shortage of cabinet space. It could be that you're simply not using existing space in the most efficient way possible. Special cabinet fittings can help you solve this problem. Many organizers are available ready-made; even more can be custom-built. On these two pages you'll see three typical custom-made cabinet maximizers that can give you ideas to make your own kitchen storage areas work better.

Behind the average cabinet or drawer front is a treasure of storage space waiting to be taken full advantage of. The drawer shown *at right,* for example, has been outfitted for small appliance storage and use—in this case, a toaster and toaster oven.

It's near the breakfast nook, so family members can make their own toast in the morning without moving around and getting in the cook's way. Eliminating the usual drawer side panels makes access to the appliances easy. And with a power outlet in the back of the drawer, there's no need to move the appliances. After use, the unit slides back out of sight on heavy-duty metal drawer glides.

If you'd like to plan a unit like this for your kitchen, make sure the drawer you use is designed without crumb-catching crevices, and with an easy-clean laminate surface.

The neatest, cleanest, best-organized kitchen has its share of trash to be discarded every day. The pullout wastebasket drawer shown *at right* makes disposing of garbage as efficient and tidy as can be.

Designed to accommodate grocery bags as liners, the trash receptacle has a plastic-laminate interior that's easy to wipe clean. Using biodegradable grocery bags as waste containers, without worrying about damage from spills and leaks, is both an economical and an ecological plus.

This unit is custom-made, but for existing cabinets you can buy accessory hardware that will let you install a standard-size plastic wastebasket into a pullout holder for the same kind of convenience.

Not all cabinets have their backs to the wall. The multipurpose island shown *at right* organizes a good part of the storage in this spacious older-home kitchen. Pullout shelves and drawers below the gas cooktop and heat-resistant ceramic tile counter store a variety of cooking utensils unobtrusively and conveniently.

Behind the sleek cabinet doors at the center of the unit are three drawers for storing cookware in the handiest possible place, right below the cooktop. Smaller drawers flanking the central section have lots of room for smaller utensils and flatware.

This kitchen has a compact and well-planned pantry cupboard, too. The double-door unit between the refrigerator and the wall ovens provides storage space for staples and packaged foods just where it's most needed—in the food preparation area.

Ready-mades that work for you

Well-outfitted storage cabinets needn't be custom-made. Several manufacturers offer cabinet units with extra features such as slide-out or revolving shelves that let you put hard-to-reach places to good use. You also can find covered drawers for bread-keeping, pullout cutting boards, and accessory hardware to do your own customizing (the hardware for making a wastebasket drawer, discussed on the opposite page, is an example).

To improve storage in your existing cabinets, look for useful accessories. Plastic, rubber, or metal grids and containers, turntables, and files can go right into your cabinets and make everything from pots and pans to cinnamon and nutmeg easier to find and reach.

The array of kitchen storage specialties on these pages is probably more than even the most clutter-ridden cook needs to sort things out, but it does give you an idea of what's in the stores for you. We've shown everything in white, on the theory that white looks good with almost any kitchen. Most of these helpers, however, come in a wide range of colors, from bright accents to warm earth-tones and wood-looks. They're as potentially decorative—and fun—as they are functional.

Because this display was designed for abundance and variety rather than exact piece-by-piece function, here's a breakdown of what might be most helpful, and where.

• *Hangables.* Grid systems, often of plastic-coated wire, let you hang items in any configuration. These systems often coordinate with similarly designed bin or shelf units for bulkier items. You also can get easy-to-mount units for the inside of closet or cabinet doors, and others that mount below existing shelves.

• *Stackables.* Stacking bins in every size multiply the usefulness of a corner, cabinet, or counter top. Some multilevel bin units have wheels and gain extra versatility from their mobility. Easily stacked canisters and dishes are a big help, too.

• *Cabinet fittings.* Look for organizers, divider units, and racks for dishes, cups, and cookware. Search out handy pullout accessories for pans, lids, or cups. And don't forget carrousel units that fit into cabinets and eliminate wasted space in hard-to-reach areas.

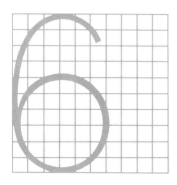

BATH STORAGE

What's in a bath? The basic fixtures—sink, tub, and toilet—of course. In addition, it's likely to have several shelves' worth of cosmetics and toiletries, cleaning supplies, miscellaneous gadgets, and—if you don't have a linen closet—stacks of towels. All this, plus the undeniable fact that most baths offer less space than any other room in the house. This chapter shows how to plan bath storage and how to find usable space where you thought there wasn't any.

PLANNING BATH STORAGE

Even if your home has more than one full bath, you may not have quite enough storage for all the varied and odd-size items you'd like to keep in them. And even where space is sufficient, you may need better organization to make things easier to locate. Start planning attractive, functional storage by asking yourself a few to-the-point questions.

What do you need?

Jot down the items you keep or would like to keep in the bath. Start with the obvious ones—toiletries, medicines, cleaning supplies, and perhaps towels and grooming accessories such as blow dryers. This is a good time to sort out and discard old, no-longer-useful medicines, dried-up shoe polish, and other odds and ends that proliferate in bathroom closets and medicine chests.

Once you take care of the basics, add some reasonable extras to your list—anything that you think would be fun or useful to have in the bath, such as a magazine rack, a telephone, or an assortment of bath crystals displayed in apothecary jars.

Make your bath as pleasant and functional as possible. Think of it as a personal work center, and assess storage priorities. What's in daily use? What do you regularly have to stop and search for? These are the things that need to be stored in the handiest place. Although accessibility is the guiding principle, safety is next: Put razors, sharp scissors, and all medicines out of the reach of children, no matter how frequently these items are used.

How can you find room?

Bath storage is much more than three cluttered medicine-chest shelves, although these shelves are the storage nucleus of just about any bathroom. Other possibilities, such as those mentioned here and detailed on the next eight pages, can help take the burden off that old standby.

• *Open storage.* If your family is basically tidy and doesn't mind putting things away in a straight line and neatly folded, this may be for you. Storing everything, particularly colorful towels and attractive cosmetics, within easy reach on open shelves or hangable or stackable modular units is both convenient and decorative.

• *Found space.* Search for unused space and put it to work. Look over, under, and next to fixtures. Seldom-used, bulky-but-not-heavy items may do well on a high shelf. Empty corners and idle floor space invite the addition of small cabinets and closets.

• *Vanities and cabinets.* You already may have a vanity and a cabinet above the sink, but are you using them to their best advantage? Are the shelves spaced for items of varying heights? Can you keep towels there, or is moisture a problem? Think of maximizing existing space and making it dry and secure enough to shelter even nonwaterproof bathroom materials.

• *Bath organizers.* You can buy a great variety of free-standing and wall-hung accessories, from soap-and-shampoo racks to counter-top towel racks just the right size for guest towels. Choose whatever colors, materials, and styles look best in your bath.

CABINETS AND VANITIES

A vanity—the cabinet that supports the standard lavatory—is probably the single most useful storage unit to have in a bath. Because it's an integral part of the sink area, it fits into the smallest room, and because it provides counter as well as cabinet space, it's multipurpose almost by definition. But you can add other cabinets to your bath—attractive wall-hung pieces above the toilet, oversize over-sink medicine chests, and drawer units that serve as chests.

Adding a ready-made vanity to a bath is an easy way to customize a standard bath fixture. Because of the wide variety of vanity styles, shapes, and sizes, you can achieve almost any effect without resorting to special-ordering or custom-building.

Prebuilt cabinets come in many finishes and materials, and with a vast array of counter options. Select tile or plastic laminate in all the colors of the rainbow, or marble or wood in a wide range of natural tones. Plastic laminate also comes as a wood-grain or marble look-alike. Durable finishes for the cabinets themselves include warm-looking wood, easy-care laminates, even canvas panels. All this means that a custom-made look is as easy as choosing the ready-made color and finish that you want.

The bath shown *opposite* offers abundant storage, all of it in prebuilt cabinets. The oak vanity and open shelves provide space for everything from towels to scouring powder, and look luxurious, as well.

If you want storage really tailored to your family's particular needs, however, you may need something customized. The custom-made cabinet shown *above,* for example, includes a pullout bin below the counter. It's an ideal laundry hamper, in an especially good position to collect clothes and towels. Ventilating holes prevent mildew.

You can individualize counter tops as well as cabinets. Often, unusual shapes, such as triangles and curves, can accommodate extra items and add design flair to a bathroom.

STANDARD VANITY SIZES

Standard prebuilt bath vanities are available in the following widths:
24"
30"
36"
42"
48"

Doors: Single or double

Drawers: Two to three. On cabinets less than 36" wide, usually on the right-hand side; on either side on larger units.

FOUND SPACE

Even a standard-issue bathroom will give up its secret hoard of underused space if you mount a determined search. Look above the toilet, around the tub, inside the walls. The treasure you're seeking may be out of sight at the moment, but you may find it just around the next fixture.

What can you store in a little space? A lot, if you plan it right and don't let corners go to waste. The 5x6-foot bathroom shown *opposite* is proof. Here, open shelving and a louvered linen closet join with the compact vanity and setback mirrored medicine cabinet to provide generous storage space.

Folded and dowel-hung items in open storage add spark to the color scheme, and as you can tell from the listing of dimensions *below, right,* folded towels don't take up much room. To hide bottles and jars, hang a shallow, shuttered closet in a corner.

The unit with glass shelves flanking the toilet tank shown *below* is an easy idea to adopt or adapt. The shelving enclosure, built of 2x4s, looks like much more work than it is. The shelves, of 3/16-inch tempered glass, mount on shelf standards and clips.

When you reclaim over-the-tank space, don't forget that you'll need to lift the tank lid occasionally, so leave space above it, or make the bottom storage shelf removable.

Keep appearances in mind, too. Here, paneling applied diagonally behind the shelves lends visual interest and depth.

The streamlined tub pictured *above* is a standard sunken model, customized with a pine surround. The surround has a hinged shelf that provides a much-needed place for soap, shampoo, and sponges. Besides providing storage space in an existing and unexpected area, this pine addition is part of a whole-bathroom remodeling that includes handsome pine built-ins below and recessed in the wall beside the lavatory.

Other places to find bath storage space include:
• Above doors.
• Directly overhead, from the ceiling.
• Under and above windows.
• At the ends of the tub.
• In corners. (Specially designed triangular shelves put this space to work.)

BATH LINEN SIZES

	Flat	Folded
Guest towels		
	11x18	5½x9
	12x20	6x10
Hand towels		
	15x26	7½x13
	16x32	8x16
	18x36	9x18
Bath towels		
	22x44	11x11
	24x48	12x12
	26x50	13x12½
	28x52	14x13
Washcloths		
	9x9	4½x9
	12x12	6x12
	14x14	7x14

Dimensions given are approximate, in inches.

BOXING IN

If you're feeling boxed in by standard bathroom fixtures, turn the tables and box *them* in. Or add boxes above or below. You'll gain storage and counter space, and a great-looking bathroom, besides.

Once you've determined the type and amount of storage you need, consider some change-of-pace methods to get that storage. If you want something less all-encompassing than a standard vanity, or don't have enough floor space for a ladder-type shelf unit like the one shown on the preceding page, think of other kinds of built-ins.

For example, the unusual long-line medicine cabinet pictured *above* replaced a standard one-door, over-the-sink unit in a tired older bathroom. The bright new unit borrows its design from the old-fashioned stack-style bookcases so popular at secondhand stores; it provides efficient, horizontal see-into storage, plus a high, wide, recessed mirror to visually maximize space. Pivot-mounted glass doors on the three storage compartments of this 4½-foot-by-12-inch-deep unit keep splashes from damaging the contents. (Note that the medicine cabinet is placed high enough above the lavatory and toilet so it doesn't interfere with the faucets and the toilet tank lid.)

The handsome wood-grain box enclosing the lavatory has two side-by-side drawers at the bottom for storing extra soap and other small items that don't lend themselves to on-view storage.

The up-to-the-minute bath pictured *opposite* shows just how far alternative thinking can take you when planning a bath from scratch. This high-tech bathroom was a sagging back porch in a turn-of-the-century house. Before adding fixtures and style, the owners bolstered, enclosed, wired, plumbed, ducted, and drywalled the porch and turned it into a room.

The extra-large, open-front, under-sink storage unit is an especially noteworthy feature. Its center compartment has lots of room for extra towels; slide-out plastic-coated baskets allow easy access. (For more about baskets and other storage components you can purchase, see the following two pages.) The two side sections are equipped with towel bars, with ample room for each person's in-use towels.

Although the vanity is custom-built and looks expensive, its price isn't in the luxury class. The tiny tiles that give the vanity its distinctive look were a closeout bargain; more of the same tiles cover the floor and tub, giving the bath a molded, one-piece look. The unusual stainless-steel twin sinks came from a dental supply company, and the hospital-style faucets from a hospital that was being dismantled.

Ample counter space between the sinks allows two people to use the sinks without bumping into each other, and also ensures sufficient counter space for surface storage.

A closet, out of camera range, provides still more space for toiletries and electrical appliances. Mirrored French doors on the closet, and the large mirror above the vanity, make the 6x13-foot space seem wider than it is.

STORAGE ACCESSORIES

Even if you don't plan to move a fixture, touch a wall, or drive more than one or two nails, a few new bath storage accessories can make a big difference. They'll dress up your bath and provide needed storage space. Hang them, slide them, stack them wherever you need room. Choose from a wide variety of materials, including painted metal, plastic-coated wire, and multihued plastic. And remember that you can use—or recycle—items not designed expressly for bath use.

Once you've decided you need portable storage pieces to bring order to your bath, you'll find them in abundance at hardware and housewares stores. For unusual finds, such as interesting magazine racks or curlicued shelves, check less obvious sources, such as secondhand stores. A coat of paint or a scrubbing can do wonders to renew a used item.

Storage units can hang individually from a shelf or ceiling, or in groups, one stacked on another. They can stand on their own, or lean against the wall. Wheel them, or just carry them from spot to spot or room to closet.

These two pages show some of the most widely available storage items. These include roll-around carts, stacking and under-shelf baskets, and shower caddies that mount from plumbing fixtures.

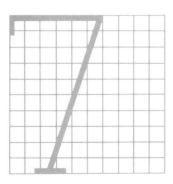

OUTFITTING CLOSETS

Some closets are catchalls, others are organized and outfitted to make use of every inch of space. Some keep clothes, others become compact offices or sewing rooms. Some are of walk-in proportions, others are mere cubbyholes. Whatever your closets are doing now, chances are they can do even more if you help them along with some extra planning, space-saving tricks, and accessories. This chapter tells how.

FOR CLOTHES STORAGE

How many favorite but faded old blouses, too-short skirts, too-tight trousers, and out-of-date ties are in your bedroom closet? Most clothes closets hold more than they have to simply because hoarding instincts keep us hanging on to things we rarely wear.

The first step in making your clothes closets work more efficiently is to ruthlessly cull your belongings. Get rid of anything you haven't worn in a year and a half. (If something has sentimental value, don't throw it out—just put it where it doesn't occupy valuable everyday storage space.)

Next, categorize your garments, putting clothes of one type together and grouping them by season. If you think it would help, you can even arrange items by color within the use categories.

Once the contents are in order, turn to the space itself. The amount of space isn't always the factor that matters most—the real key is how space is used. A well-equipped closet should provide three specific types of storage:
• Hanging space for long items.
• Double hanging space to allow for two tiers of separates.
• Space for folded items.

The room-size closet pictured *at right* does all this on a grand scale. Rods line both walls. A center island stores folded items and provides a surface convenient for arranging outfits that work well. Track lighting and an extra-wide, full-length mirror let the owners get really good looks at themselves. Most closets aren't this spacious, but refitting them as explained on the following pages can make them work as if they were.

(continued)

CLOTHING SPACE NEEDS

LENGTH IN INCHES

Long dresses	69
Regular dresses	45
Skirts	35
Trousers (cuff-hung)	44
Trousers (double-hung)	20
Blouses and shirts	28
Women's suits	29
Men's suits	38
Ties	27
Coats	50-52
Dress bags	48
Travel bags	41
Garment bags	57
Hanging shoe bags	36
Wooden hangers	21
Plastic hangers	17

● You need 8 inches of rod length for every ten shirts or blouses to be hung.

● A top shelf is usually 84 inches high, which often leaves room for another shelf below that one.

If your closet won't accommodate two permanent rods, buy lower rods that hang from the existing top rod, or improvise by hanging a lower rod from the top rod with chains.

Use vertical closet space, too. Even ceiling space is usable if you construct a storage box and attach it to the ceiling with hinges on one side. Lower it with a pulley arrangement when you want to reach it.

Make door space count by replacing bifold or sliding doors with hinged doors that offer an inside surface for mounting storage racks or hooks.

Thanks to drawers and open shelves, the two customized closets shown here have lots of room for boys' sports and hobby equipment as well as clothes. Even if you don't plan to store items other than clothes in your closets, a drawer unit or cabinet is a good idea. It at least partly eliminates the need for storage furniture in the bedroom itself, and it keeps everything you need for dressing in one convenient area.

To find out precisely how much closet space you need, do some experimenting on paper. Here are several basic dimensions to help you plan your closet.

● A typical closet rod is 67 to 69 inches above the floor and 12 to 14 inches from the wall.

● If you use two closet rods, place the top one at 76 to 84 inches above the floor, the lower one at 36 to 42 inches.

FOR OTHER USES

Closets can be the life of the party when they're outfitted to hold entertaining essentials such as glassware, linens, serving pieces—even beverages. Existing closets are easily converted to store party and dining supplies. Or start from the beginning, designing specialized storage near your kitchen or dining room. Either way, you may find that a well-planned serving closet is a household asset second only to having a butler.

There are as many approaches to storing glassware, tableware, and party supplies as there are styles of entertaining. In some situations, drawers might be the answer; in others, shelves.

In the room shown in the photo *at upper left*, two identical closets are equipped to store tableware and glassware. Deep slide-out drawers on steel glides hold goblets, serving dishes, pitchers, platters, and other often-used items. Above the drawers, two fixed shelves house less-frequently used pieces.

The closet shown *at lower left* was once an awkward corner of a kitchen; now it's a storage center for china and linen. Shelves in the closet itself are used for linens and other bulky items. Glassware is held securely and conveniently in place on 4½-inch-deep shelves mounted on the inside of the doors.

The entry hall closet pictured *opposite* is an even more welcoming sight as a serving center than it was as a place to hang coats and hats. Here, the space is dressed up with a redwood counter topped with a mirrored back and side walls. Glass shelves, supported by 2½-inch dowels, hold glassware; the cabinets below keep bottles, ice buckets, and additional glasses.

If you're planning glassware storage, these dimensions should help you.
• Space shelves 6 inches apart for cordial and old-fashioned glasses.
• Space shelves 10 inches apart for wine-, champagne, beer, and highball glasses.
• Space shelves 14 inches apart for pilsner and tall-stemmed brandy glasses.

FOR A
SEWING CENTER

The sewing center you've always wanted may be just a closet conversion away. If your needs are very simple, you can probably slip your machine and some shelves into an existing closet. If you want something a bit more elaborate, you may want to custom-tailor the space and furnish it with a work surface and ample fabric storage.

The sewing center shown *opposite* proves that you can outfit even a very small space super-efficiently. It accommodates a drop-down worktable, sewing machine, and fabric storage on dowel rods—all on the back of the closet door. Inside the closet itself are a recessed wastebasket, slanted thread storage, cubbyholes for additional fabric storage, and wall-mounted perforated hardboard for storing scissors and notions. A mirror and hanging bar on the back wall make this ingenious sewing center as practical as can be.

The work surface in this deluxe sewing closet is carefully engineered. It, and its three supporting legs, are hinged to the stationary ledge that houses the sewing machine. The machine is permanently parked there, but when the table folds up against the fabric storage area and the door is closed, the whole unit fits into the closet.

If you want something even more compact, the arrangement shown *at right* may be just what you're looking for. The sewing desk is tucked into what was once an open storage niche in the family room—between an outer wall and the lower-level chimney base of a first-floor fireplace.

After the freestanding machine was moved into place, a pair of shelves was added above it to store fabric, patterns, and other supplies. Hooks in a scrap of plywood beside the machine hold scissors. A fluorescent tube mounted to the underside of the lower shelf provides good sewing light. Double doors were added so that the sewing corner could be out of the way during parties or family activities.

OUTFITTING CLOSETS

FOR A HOME OFFICE

Working at home doesn't have to mean settling for cardboard files and a wobbly card-table desk. A home office can be every bit as attractive as any corporate quarters. And it doesn't require a lot of space; it's possible to keep office hours in a closet. Scout the closets in your guest room, family room, even your own bedroom. You can keep your desk work behind doors or, if you're a neat worker, remove all vestiges of the closet and merge it with the rest of the room.

Like other offices, a home office is basically composed of two elements—storage space and work surfaces. Depending on the kind of work you do, you'll probably need one type of space more than another. First determine how your workplace will function, then assess the space that's available.

The well-equipped home office pictured *at left* makes its home in the guest room's former closet. After the doors, closet pole, and header were removed, a birch-faced plywood storage system was put into place. The laminate-top desk and cabinet unit still doubles as a vanity for guests, but during business hours it's home base for a typewriter, telephone, and office supplies.

If your own work calls for more surface space than the office in this photo, you might want to plan pullout tables to supplement the desk top. Make sure the desk top is sturdy and level, particularly if you use a typewriter, computer, or other equipment.

Office storage needs are likely to be fairly straightforward. Plan for bookshelves, files, and, perhaps, cabinet space for materials such as paper. Make sure you have at least one drawer for small office supplies, and look for desk-top stackables to give you maximum storage in minimum space.

Office accessories that can help you keep the area neat include stacking drawer units, stacking plastic bins, modular drawer organizers, storage baskets or trays to use on shelves or in roll-around carts, and plastic file boxes.

JUST FOR KIDS

Children are rarely orderly by nature, or even tall enough to use adult-size closets, so standard closet space may not be the ideal storage solution for children's rooms. Think of what your youngsters have to store, then imagine trying to fit toys, games, and miniature clothing items into your own closet. You may decide more appropriate storage possibilities are in order—and you'll find several on these pages.

To be really good, storage space needs to match the items to be stored and the size of the person doing the storing. For children, that often means horizontal storage at their own level rather than typical vertical closet space. It also means storage that's convenient to use—and adaptable enough to house everything from party dresses to hockey sticks.

Devising storage that meets these special needs sometimes requires a little imagination. For example, the repainted old school lockers shown *at upper right* have been made even more practical with additional shelves; they're perfect for both toys and clothes. Look for cast-off lockers in schools, gyms, or sports clubs that are being remodeled or dismantled.

For even more flexible storage, think of a creative do-it-yourself project. It doesn't take advanced skills to re-create the ingenious storage area pictured *at lower right*. First, support a wooden ladder—this one is 10 feet long—with a three-sided structure of wooden strips. Then, sew (or purchase and adapt) pouches of colorful, sturdy fabric—canvas in this case. Finally, attach the pouches along the sides and sling them over the ladder rails.

If you're looking for ideas for a more elaborate storage system, study the picture *opposite.* The shallow, many-shelved storage unit in the center was built in front of a brick chimney. It's flanked by deeper units that have ample room for clothes and toys. The side shown here includes a mirror, bureau drawers, and side shelves; the other houses a closet with low, child-height poles. All hide neatly behind sleek flush doors.

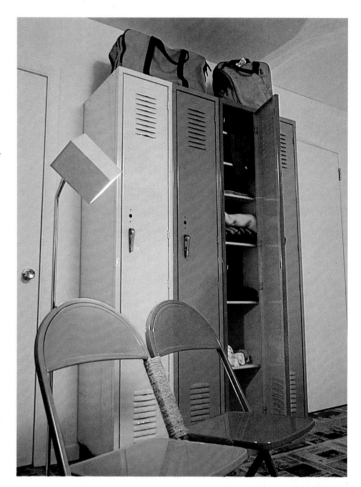

OUTFITTING CLOSETS

CLOSET ACCESSORIES

To help you create order out of chaos—or keep chaos from developing in the first place—manufacturers have devised a wide variety of closet accessories. They range from whole-closet systems to simple hooks and racks. Many adjust or adapt to the particular closet configuration you're working with. And best of all, these organizers are usually inexpensive— small investments with a large return.

Custom-fitting a closet doesn't require a lot of skill, especially if you *buy* the fittings rather than build them. The storage systems and products shown *at right*—and more like them— can help you tailor a closet almost instantly.

Taking center stage in the photo is a wooden shelf system with rods. This easy-to-assemble prepackaged unit is available in various sizes to turn just about any storage space into a first-class closet.

At the right of the photo are combination shelves and rods. These units are available in 12- and 16-inch depths, and can be cut to fit any length up to 12 feet. Adjustable bars with snap-in nylon hanger glides are another closet-rod option. For twice the hanging space, buy double rods.

To accommodate folded clothes, shoes, and small items of clothing neatly, look to bins, baskets, boxes, or racks like the ones shown at the lower left of the photo. Stacking plastic bins make a colorful and convenient display for sweaters or scarves. Slide-out wire trays in an open frame, wheeled carts containing three or four wire-mesh stacking baskets, and wall-mounted swing bins provide mobility as well as space. And don't overlook such versatile everyday items as plastic boxes, milk crates, and vegetable bins.

For narrow back-of-the-door space, use metal door racks with adjustable shelves, or a wire grid system with snap-on hooks. Mount a wire hook rack on the door or sidewall for more storage. Finally, don't forget about those familiar but still-practical and space-efficient multiple hangers for trousers, shirts, ties, and belts.

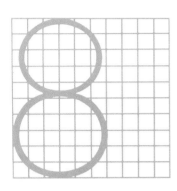

SPECIALTY STORAGE

Crafting, woodworking, laundering, sewing, collecting wine—special activities demand specialized storage. In this chapter you'll find six roomfuls of storage custom-tailored for special activities. Borrow or adapt these ideas to make the best possible use of the special-purpose areas at your house.

LAUNDRY CENTERS

Do you wait to do laundry until you have nothing left to wear? And when you do get around to it, do you find yourself wasting steps and time? A well-organized laundry center may not completely rid you of the washday blues, but it can streamline the task.

Because a washer and dryer take up a substantial amount of space, plan your laundry storage around them. At the very least, you'll want a shelf near the washer for storing detergents and other supplies and a table near the dryer for folding and sorting. Especially if you don't have a separate laundry room, you may want to build these features into cabinetry in order to keep them out of sight when they're not in use. Be sure to allow enough room so that both top- and front-loading machines have clearance.

The 11x14-foot laundry room shown *at right* was customized to meet three goals, only one of them laundry-related. Simplified, efficient clothes care shares space with dried-flower arranging and preparing food for freezing. Many of the features are equally suitable for a laundry that is not going to serve such diverse needs.

Doors and drawers screen a series of carefully planned storage units. These include a pulldown ironing board, extra-deep 22-inch drawers, and two sorting bins (one for dirty laundry, the other for items awaiting ironing). A closet bar in an alcove provides a convenient place for air-drying permanent press items and hanging just-ironed clothing. Laminated counters provide ample surfaces for stacking and folding clean laundry. Opposite this wall, out of camera range, are the washer, dryer, and freezer. *(continued)*

Y ou don't have to banish your laundry center to the outer reaches of the house. Clean-lined closed storage and built-in appliances provide an efficient laundry that's attractive enough to be part of your home's main living area. And in an easily accessible spot, a multipurpose laundry earns its keep even when it's not washday.

Wash time and party time are not mutually exclusive in this combination laundry/refreshment area. Built into an old pantry, the center is adjacent to the home's kitchen and dining room and just a few steps from the family room. The convenient location and the family's casual entertaining style helped them decide to combine a laundry with a serving area and wet bar.

The photo *at left* shows the working laundry. Base cabinet doors swing open to reveal the dryer, and sections of the counter top and backsplash open with piano hinges and fold to expose the washer and the appliances' control panels. Ample cabinets below the sink stow detergents and other supplies neatly out of sight.

Closing the cabinets and folding down the laminate counter hide all traces of the laundry center. When it's time to entertain, the wash sink becomes a bar sink, the counter a serving surface, and glasses and other party supplies come out of the upper cabinets.

For still more convenience, you could install an under-counter refrigerator to keep beverages and ice.

An easily concealed laundry like this one is an ideal solution when you have to locate your laundry in the kitchen. The counter space you use for folding towels in the morning will serve just as well for preparing dinner in the evening.

NUMBERS TO KNOW

Washers and dryers
Side-by-side units typically take up 48 to 56 inches of wall space and are about 28 inches deep, with a 34- to 36-inch-high work surface. Stacking units range from 24 to 28 inches wide and stand about 72 inches high. Because stacking washers are front-loaders, they also work well for side-by-side, under-counter installations.

Sinks
Full-size laundry tubs are big—up to 48 inches wide for double-well versions—and probably not imperative in this age of machine-washable fabrics. Sinks for pretreating stains and washing delicate items range in size from 21 to 33 inches wide by about 24 inches front to back. Compact, extra-deep sinks—13½ inches square by 15½ inches deep—also are useful for bathing babies or potting plants.

Freezers
Upright models are typically 66 inches high, 29 to 33 inches wide, and 29 to 32 inches deep; chest freezers are 26 to 71 inches long, about 28 inches wide, and about 36 inches high (you'll need an additional 28 inches clearance above for opening the freezer).

CRAFT ROOMS

It's hard for any craft to be an important part of your life if supplies and equipment are tucked away in an inaccessible place. A craft center may help you enjoy your craft more—and more often. Good organization and a convenient place to put everything are important both in full-fledged craft centers and in rooms that are also used for other activities. Ideally, a craft center combines an uncluttered work surface with ample closed and open storage—closed to conceal clutter and open, where it's suitable, to turn storage space into gallery space for works in progress.

The needlecraft room pictured *at right* features highly specialized storage. A compartmentalized shelving unit keeps an assortment of colored yarns sorted at all times. An upright wooden ladder, made from vertically placed oak 2x4s and horizontal dowel rods, displays an inviting array of yard goods. Below the ladder, craft accessories find a temporary resting place in a deep wicker basket. Behind the ladder, a cork wall keeps sketches and unfinished projects close at hand.

Your craft may require more closed storage than we've shown here. If so, include closets, cabinets, and shelving in your plan. Keep in mind that closed storage is essential if your craft uses tools or chemicals that should be kept away from young children. To make sure everything will fit, make a list of the items you'll be storing and note their dimensions.

If you need a sink in your craft room, find out which wall (if any) encloses existing plumbing. Locating a sink where it can tap into a "wet wall" is the easiest and least expensive alternative. Positioning cupboards and counter space near the sink will boost efficiency.

Consider, too, the amount of counter or table surface you'll need. Pottery-making, for example, requires more work surface than model building.

Because work performed in a craft room frequently requires close and constant eye contact, good lighting is a must. Take advantage of any natural light and supplement it with artificial lighting. Your storage facilities won't be convenient if you have to grope around dark cupboards or closets to find your supplies, so make sure that these areas, too, are well lit.

SEWING ROOMS

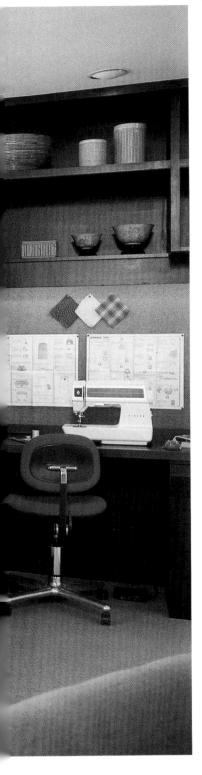

Your sewing room doesn't have to be enclosed by four walls. Often, it's more feasible to set up a sewing center in a corner or along one wall of a larger room. But good storage is vital wherever you do your sewing. Equipment and supplies should be readily accessible, yet—particularly in a sewing center that's part of another room—unobtrusive when you're not sewing. Appropriate closed storage lets you stow everything out of sight between sewing sessions. You'll want a well-lit space with ample surfaces to spread out lengths of fabric. And keep in mind that even a portable sewing machine is quite heavy, so try to install yours in a convenient and fairly permanent spot.

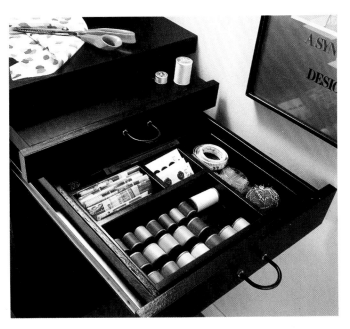

In the super-organized center shown *at left,* everything has its place. The sewing machine rests on a laminated counter top. Behind it, carpeting on the wall makes a handy eye-level bulletin board for instructions. To keep your machine out of sight when it's not being used, consider building it into its own cabinet, attaching it to a flip-up table, or screening it with a shade, curtain, or mini-slat blind.

The surface your machine rests on should stand about 30 inches high and be large enough to allow you to rest your arms while feeding fabric through the machine. Corners should be rounded so that material won't snag on them.

Near the machine, allow space for lots of sewing accessories. Here, closed cabinets, and a bank of compartmentalized drawers, shown *above,* keep needles, thread spools, measuring tools, chalk, and scissors in order and within easy reach. If you prefer open storage, wall-hung shelving and perforated

hardboard are other efficient catchalls.

Remember, too, to include hanging storage for works in progress as well as for keeping fabric wrinkle-free. Here, a closet with a full-length mirror holds clothing and ironing supplies. You may prefer a built-in, fold-down ironing board.

Conserving space

When space is tight, it's often hard to provide a large, smooth surface for laying out patterns and cutting fabric. Here, the solution was a handy pullout cutting table made from a folding tabletop attached to a rollable box at the front. The box does more than support the table; dowels mounted from an open-bottom drawer neatly store yard goods. In its closed position the box is flush with the cabinets, and a hinged section of the tabletop pulls up to conceal the shelves. At left, a stacking washer and dryer use only half the horizontal space needed for a conventional side-by-side arrangement.

SPECIALTY STORAGE

SHOPS

Having work space for repairs, carpentry projects, or other tool-oriented pastimes is one of the great satisfactions of owning a home. Where you locate a shop depends partly on access (can you easily bring in bulky materials such as 4x8-foot sheets of plywood and long boards?) and partly on isolation (you'll want to keep dust, fumes, and noise out of the rest of the house). In most homes, the basement is the likeliest spot, but you may prefer to set up shop in the garage or in a backyard shed. Organizing a shop and providing safe, convenient storage for everything that belongs there is just as important as finding the space itself. On this page we'll give you some pointers that can help you put tools and materials in their rightful places.

Whether your shop is as elaborate as the converted garage shown *at left* or consists of just a simple bench and a few shelves, the same general storage advice applies.

A stationary workbench can provide counters and drawers underneath and perforated hardboard hanging places above. In a bigger shop or one that's used for other purposes, a roll-around bench may give you more flexibility.

For storing small hand tools, perforated hardboard is ideal. For nails, nuts, and other easily mislaid and missorted items, get an organizer filled with small plastic drawers. Wall-mount it or place it on a counter or shelf. Plastic food containers can accommodate larger items. Labeling is especially important when you have lots of containers filled with lots of little things.

Bigger items, because they're harder to lose track of, don't require the same painstaking containerization that small gadgets and hardware do, but lost or misplaced tools are big time-wasters. To keep tools at hand, follow these principles.

• A tool should be easy to put away. If you have convenient storage, you'll tend to set the tool where it belongs.

• Tools should be protected in storage. Sheathe or suspend edges so they don't dull.

• Tools should be stored in relation to each other—wrenches with other wrenches and pliers, saws with other wood cutting tools—so everything comes to hand naturally.

For materials such as lumber or plywood, dry storage is essential, but it needn't be right at hand. For example, you might suspend brackets from ceiling rafters for overhead storage of bulky items.

SPECIALTY STORAGE

WINE CELLARS

Whether you're a serious collector of interesting vintages or just like to keep a case or two of your favorite wines on hand, you've probably had to give some thought to how to store your wine. Good storage at controlled temperatures is vital to preserving the quality of just about any wine. Here are some ideas for providing that kind of storage in your home.

A wine cellar doesn't have to be a stone basement, or even a facility as elaborate as the one shown here. The first thing you need is a space big enough to rack as many bottles as you'd like to keep on hand. If you buy only a few bottles at a time, your "cellar" might be nothing more than the bottom shelf of a kitchen cabinet, or a purchased rack on a bookshelf.

But if you prefer to buy wines in quantity, you'll need not only more space, but the right kind of space. Extensive storage is long-term storage; and wine can deteriorate if conditions aren't right.

First, make sure the location you choose is out of direct sunlight. Otherwise, your wines could spoil, and the reds may lose their color.

Strive to maintain a temperature in your cellar of 55 to 65 degrees Fahrenheit. Avoid locations, such as the kitchen, where temperatures are likely to fluctuate more than a few degrees. Similarly, stay away from places where vibrations often occur, such as a laundry. Movement can damage a wine's delicate chemistry.

Storage units include racks, wall-hung compartmentalized shelving, and floor-to-ceiling units. Whatever arrangement you choose, racks should allow you to store bottles on their sides. Wine keeps the corks moist and prevents shrinking, which could let air into the bottle and spoil the wine.

Redwood lumber, terra-cotta tile, and pine lath provide an attractive and functional ambience in the wine cellar/ tasting room pictured *at right*. Fiber-glass insulation stapled between the wall studs and around the heater enclosure helps maintain an even temperature.

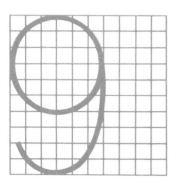

OUTDOOR STORAGE

A storage place as big as all outdoors may sound like the answer to all your storage problems, but space alone is not enough. Organization is at least as important. Gardening, outdoor cooking and entertaining, and family activities go more smoothly when the items you need are properly stored so they're ready when you are. In this chapter, we give you storage ideas for everything from barbecue equipment and bicycles to garbage cans and garden tools.

GREENHOUSES

If your family includes an avid gardener, plants, potting supplies, gardening tools, and chemicals and sprays can accumulate until they demand a place of their own. A greenhouse in either an even-span or lean-to design answers both gardening and storage needs. An even-span greenhouse is a complete unit that stands on its own; a lean-to attaches to an existing structure.

If you're looking for a place for spring potting and winter storage of gardening equipment, an unheated even-span unit such as the one shown on these pages is all you'll need. This inexpensive and easy-to-assemble design can be built by a reasonably skilled do-it-yourselfer in just a couple of weekends. The greenhouse offers two roomy potting shelves, hanging-basket supports, and floor space for large plants, shrubs, supplies, and tools.

Two screen doors and adjustable ceiling vents permit ventilation and humidity control. The unit is framed with pressure-treated lumber; basket-weave-type fencing forms the arched roof structure. Plastic sheeting stapled to the framework covers the roof.

For glazing a structure of this type, you'll need to use glass, fiber glass, or acrylic panels. If you plan to use the greenhouse year round, a lean-to style may be more economical. Because it attaches to a wall of your house, you can tap into heating and electrical systems already in place.

SHEDS

Is your garage a tangle of lawn mowers, trash cans, bicycles, barbecue equipment, sports gear, and garden tools? Is the family car spending winters out in the cold so these items can stay snug inside? If so, you may be ready for a backyard shed to handle the overflow. A shed can bring order to outdoor living and ease the storage squeeze on other areas of your home. And the right design can enhance outdoor entertaining in the process.

A backyard shed doesn't have to be a drab, prefabricated outbuilding, and it can do a lot more than just store tools. The two examples shown here prove that a shed can look good and serve a variety of functions.

When planning your storage shed, think about your total outdoor living needs. Do you have a comfortable spot for entertaining, sunning, cooking out, or relaxing? Would you like to block an unsightly view or gain more privacy?

The unusual two-for-one design shown *above* illustrates how an imaginative plan can solve many problems. One side offers lockable storage for garden equipment and outdoor cooking utensils. The other half is an open-air entertainment area sheltered enough to be enjoyed rain or shine. The three-sided, covered outdoor retreat adjoins the deck.

Both the storage and seating areas are wired for lighting fixtures. Recessed heating units in the ceiling take the chill off rainy days or evenings. Insects aren't a problem where this house is located, but in other areas you may need screens to keep the area free of bugs. If security is a concern, you might want to add solid sliding doors or removable panels to enclose the living area when it's not in use.

A shed can be freestanding or attached to a house, garage, or carport—but however it's built, it should harmonize with its surroundings. Keep the structure in scale with the house and yard, and choose a design that complements rather than competes with the architectural styling of your home. Although a shed can be usefully sited almost anywhere, check zoning ordinances for minimum setback distances from property lines.

The versatile cedar shed/deck combination shown *above* offers secure storage and an outdoor entertaining area. Half of the 11x12-foot structure serves as a mini-porch for waiting out a shower or taking a shady siesta; the enclosed portion provides a place to park the lawn mower and other yard equipment. Elevated a foot or so above grade, the 20-foot-wide cedar deck serves as a pavilion for the shed and offers plenty of room for sunning or dining al fresco.

The porch can be closed completely by sliding three big panels together, barn-door-style. Come nightfall or a rainstorm, move the furniture inside the porch, secure panels from the inside, and exit by the back door of the shed. In winter, the porch becomes an extension of the shed for off-season storage.

The shed employs a combination of 2x4 stud framing and post-and-beam construction. Walls and roof are sheathed in exterior-grade plywood, and finished with cedar siding and shakes.

UNEXPECTED PLACES

Looking for the room and convenience of a shed in an unobtrusive package? Consider camouflaging outdoor storage space in a double-duty structure. Here, a modular fence keeps yard equipment neatly out of sight. On the following pages we'll show you a deck that works hard below-deck too, and a paneled cabana that also stows garden and pool supplies.

The multipurpose fence, shown open and closed on these pages, provides privacy for the yard, along with shelter for bulky mowers and other equipment. It also offers ample shelving for small tools, hoses, potting supplies, and garden sprays. What's more, this fence is tall enough to screen an unsightly view, if that's a problem in your yard.

The modular stow-it-all fence design features five individual 3-foot-wide units set side by side on pressure-treated 4x8 footings. The rest of the project is constructed of 2x4 framing and 1x8 and 1x4 boards. You can build as many modules as you need now, then add more units later.

With all doors closed, *upper left,* the storage aspect of the fence is scarcely noticeable. The first module (see photo *at lower left*) opens from the end, so you can easily maneuver a lawn mower in and out. The lower half of the wall between this and the adjacent module is open to accommodate different mower sizes and handle configurations, as you can see in the photo *opposite.*

Additional modules feature shelves for small tools and vertical tool storage with hooks and hangers. A lockable overhead cabinet in the far right portion of the photo *opposite* safely stores garden sprays and insecticides.

When selecting the site for any storage structure, choose a location that's convenient and easily accessible for gardening and yard work, but avoid using a prime spot that would be better for play space, planting, or sunning.

UNEXPECTED PLACES
(continued)

This modular deck features lift-up panels that conceal horizontal storage space beneath the surface. You can tuck away garden and yard tools, hoses, and other paraphernalia in these hidden compartments built of pressure-treated lumber and plywood.

The storage units are floored with 1x4 slatted bottoms for good ventilation and drainage. Leave ¼- to ½-inch spaces between slats. The plywood surfaces can be finished with a weather-resistant coating to help moisture-proof the compartments. Slope the top surface for drainage and place the deck over a gravel bed.

The two-part cabana pictured *opposite* packs a storage compartment and dressing room into one compact structure. It has plenty of shelves for garden supplies and chemicals on one side, and the changing booth (see inset) serves as a storage area before and after the pool season. Each side has an exterior door for convenient access.

The 4x4-foot unit is built with panels of rough-sawn exterior plywood siding with decorative trim. A mini mansard-style roof is capped with an acrylic skylight to brighten the changing area. Awnings extend from the sloping roof sides to cut down the sun's heat inside, keeping bathers as well as any temperature-sensitive chemicals from overheating.

OPEN-AIR KITCHENS

With all the supplies at your fingertips, a backyard barbecue can be a welcome spur-of-the-moment event. The secret is good organization. Here we show two approaches—a cart that makes summer dining a movable feast, and an outdoor cooking center that keeps the chef outside where the action is.

One step-saving cart can be worth a thousand trips to the kitchen. The attractive indoor/outdoor barbecue cart shown *above* will earn its keep year round. Load it with picnic goodies, then roll it out on the deck or patio to serve as a mobile buffet table. Or fire up the hibachi and cook right on the durable laminated top of the unit. When winter comes, roll the cart inside and use it as a portable bar or tea caddy.

Ample storage underneath keeps all of your barbecue supplies organized and close at hand. You can store a small grill, charcoal, and lighter fluid in the large cupboard. Tool pegs on the inside of the door keep utensils handy.

Four drawers, two on each side, are equipped with dividers to house flatware, napkins and linens, spices, matches, and condiments. Beneath the drawers, shelves are open on both sides of the cart for quick access to beverages, food, dishes, and glassware.

Make it yourself
You can build this cart with just two sheets of ½-inch exterior-grade plywood. Two pairs of 10-inch wheels, connected with 1-inch dowel axles, get it rolling. Top the cart with plastic laminate or a heat-resistant tile surface. Fill exposed plywood edges with wood filler, and paint the cart with exterior semigloss paint.

ummer entertaining and family gatherings can be more fun if the cook is part of the festivities. A permanent outdoor food preparation area could be the solution.

A cookout center should be a good-looking and functional work area. Locate it near the outdoor dining area on your deck or patio, but not too far from the kitchen.

Whether you use a built-in gas or electric barbecue, a portable charcoal grill or hibachi, or the classic brick barbecue pit, the grill is the key element of your cookout center. The type of grill helps determine the site, especially if you must run wiring or a gas line to the area. Consult an electrician or plumber for assistance if needed, and use only electrical materials approved for outdoor use.

Plan your storage around the grill, providing plenty of shelving and cupboards for utensils, condiments, spices, linens, and serving items.

The handy barbecue area shown *at left* features a bench built of 2x6s with slanting 2x4 supports to provide a seating and serving surface. For durability, build your cook center out of cedar, redwood, or exterior-grade plywood. Laminate or tile work surfaces will stand up to the weather. Seal all wood surfaces with a clear or opaque stain, exterior paint, or sealant to ensure long life and easy care.

ODDS AND ENDS

Even the best-groomed yard's appearance can be spoiled by unsightly trash cans, scattered tools, or bicycles lying around haphazardly. Attention to proper storage for odds and ends helps keep your yard looking good; it also eliminates the annoyance of looking for lost tools, tripping over downed bikes, or cleaning up garbage after marauding animals. Here are some ideas to help you tidy up the yard.

If you waste gardening time hunting for the rake, hoe, or trowel, a garden truck could save you time and steps. This deluxe-looking version is basically a wheeled box with a hinged lid. For a small investment in time and money, you'll get a big payoff in convenience: The caddy will carry your gear where you need it and keep it orderly for easy storage.

First buy a basic hand truck (a used one will cost less), then build the box and mount it on the hand truck with bolts. To build the box, you'll need 1½ sheets of ¾-inch A-C exterior plywood and eight linear feet of 1x2s. Hinge the top on one side with two 2-inch hinges. Then attach metal straps over wood blocks on the side to form a tool rack. Finish with exterior paint or stain. For super-efficient storage inside the box, install dividers to separate the interior space into bins and tool sections.

Here's an inventive way to screen the inevitable trash cans from view— a double-opening redwood bin. It gives easy access to can lids through lightweight, upward-opening hinged doors on top; below, doors open to allow the cans to slide out easily. The bins are lined with washable galvanized sheet metal, and a concrete floor slopes so it drains quickly after hosing. The doors and lids are built with redwood boards. Use 1-inch-thick flush braced frames behind, covered with sheet metal. Frame the lids with 2x3s.

Bicycles pose a special storage problem because they come in many sizes and one standard, unwieldy shape. Adults may be conscientious about properly storing expensive touring bikes in the garage or shed. But what can you do to end the obstacle course of kids' bikes scattered across the lawn or driveway?

The simple and effective solution shown *at left* is ideal for year-round bicycle storage in dry climates. Elsewhere, consider it a way to unclutter the summertime scene outdoors. It's a bike rack you don't see until you need it. This in-ground system takes up little space. You can build it in a narrow side yard, adjacent to the driveway or next to a garage or carport. Just be sure it's convenient to an entry so children will see and use it.

To build the storage rack, first line an oblong pit with gravel, sand, or bark chips. The dimensions of both the pit and the rack will depend on how many bikes you plan to store in the rack.

Redwood, cedar, or pressure-treated lumber are the best choices for the rack, because they are the most weather- and decay-resistant materials. Use two long 2x2s to frame the rack; then nail the rest of the 2x2s at right angles to the frame. Lay down the 2x2s with 1 inch between, except for the wheel-holder slots. Build these with 2-inch spacers. Set the wheel slots 2 feet apart to allow room for the handlebars.

For year-round storage that's protected from wind, snow, and rain, build a lean-to over the rack. Add lockable doors to provide security.

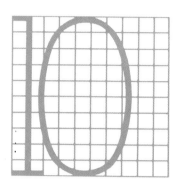

10
STORAGE SURPRISES

Just when you think you've exhausted every square inch of storage space in your house, you may discover an additional sliver of wall, an extra peg, an underused closet shelf, or an unassuming piece of furniture waiting to be put to use. If you're looking for storage in unexpected places, this chapter will help you in your search and guide you to a decision about how best to use the space once you find it.

AS DECOR

Not all storage has to be discreetly hidden away. Many functional, everyday items are good-looking enough to be stored in plain sight. For example, a ceiling-hung basket collection adds country charm to the room pictured *at left; above,* jewelry, belts, and other fashion accessories form a creative montage on a bedroom wall.

When you find space on walls, doors, or ceilings that's suitable for storing decorative items, simple hardware and housewares accessories can help you secure and display them. Good storage possibilities include:

• Glass shelves to use across windows.

• Wire racks on walls.

• Good-looking boxes or baskets stacked on the floor.

• Clear plastic boxes to show off colorful fabrics or yarns.

• Perforated hardboard with metal hooks to store cookware and utensils attractively and within easy reach.

UNDER STAIRS

Storage potential is likely to escalate when you consider the area under stairs, whether those stairs lead to the basement, attic, or between floors. The secret to turning this region into functioning space is organization. With planning and careful (sometimes custom) fitting of drawers, shelves, bins, and racks, you can pack as much into an underused under-the-stairs area as you can into the largest conventional closet. If you've got the stairs but need ideas, the stairway storage spaces on these two pages may help you step-up your own storage-finding program.

Any house with a stairway has built-in storage space just waiting to be used. The space under basement stairs is an especially good candidate for conversion to orderly storage. Whether your basement doubles as a family room, laundry, hobby center, or is just a big, open, cluttered storage space in its own right, you're likely to need a place to put things.

The storage facilities in the basement family room pictured *opposite*—practically a one-family community recreation center—show just how far good planning can take you. Where the stairs offer the most height, tall, slim pullouts house fishing poles and skis. Bulkier items, such as sleeping bags and life jackets, are stored in a roomy closet. In the spaces at the bottom of the stairway, a pair of pullout boxes houses assorted smaller items.

With pullout compartments set on heavy-duty casters, sliding the storage units in and out is easy. Perforated hardboard offers hanging space, and shelves and bins hold balls, skates, and other recreational equipment.

Basements aren't the only places with stairway nooks and crannies. The old-time closet under the stairs in the front hall is as good an idea as ever. New design concepts also offer creative approaches to under-stair storage. The rainbow-brightened corner shown *below* is the storage center of a teenager's remodeled two-level room. Stairs lead to a sleeping loft, and under-stair space is packed with storage ideas, including banks of drawers for clothes and custom-fitted shelves for books, tapes, and collectibles.

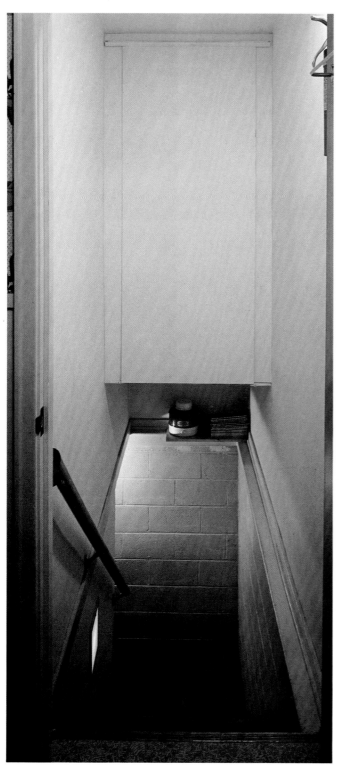

Storage space doesn't have to be huge to be effective. In pint-size places such as halls, you can create a surprising amount of storage. Imagination and planning are the keys. Here are three clever hallway hideaways.

If you've ever doubted that your home is your castle, here's a modern-day drawbridge you can install. But instead of keeping knights errant on their side of the moat, it gives you access to unexpected storage space.

The off-season storage closet shown *opposite* is built into the end wall above the basement stairs and reached by way of the door, which turns into a drawbridge when you pull it down. A long pole hook lets you pull on the iron strip at the top of the door. Then a cable-and-pulley system, with a large counterbalancing weight, lowers the walkway.

The "gangplank" shown here was made of a frame of 2x4s, faced with ½-inch plywood on both sides. Fully open, the gangplank rests on the stairway's top step. Rubberized stair treads ensure a secure footing.

Two sides to every door

If your home has a back hallway and you are not bound by the belief that storage space must be concealed, you may well find a bonanza near the back door. The rear entry pictured *above, left,* offers a variety of solutions to the problem of tight storage space.

Attractive natural wood boards equipped with hooks provide coat storage in a spot where a conventional closet would be impossible. Rubberized metal shelving, wall-mounted next to the back steps, keeps canned goods, packaged foods, and condiments within easy reach of the kitchen. On the opposite wall, an oak cabinet holds necessary but less aesthetically pleasing items such as cleaning supplies.

A more centrally located main- or second-floor hallway also may offer unexpected storage space. The add-in closet *above, right,* makes excellent use of the end of a hall. Here, a pair of vinyl-clad wood-core bookshelves was joined with a continuous piano hinge. The back shelves were anchored to the hallway wall and casters were fastened to the base of the front shelves so the closet door could swing easily. To camouflage the addition, the exterior was upholstered with the same carpet used on the hall floor.

ON THE
CEILING

When walls have yielded all the storage space they can muster, look up. Every room or hallway has a ceiling that's probably doing little more than supporting a light fixture. Why not put it to work? Just make sure your ceiling storage system is firmly secured with toggle bolts or hollow wall anchors, and is sturdy enough to support the weight of whatever you're storing.

The accessibility of ceiling storage depends on two things: the height of the ceiling and the depth of the storage system. Some ceiling storage may be just the right place to tuck away off-season items that will be retrievable only by step stool. Or you may want an easy-to-reach display of colorful cookware.

The added-on storage rafters shown *opposite* are within reach of most cooks—and building them is a task within reach of most weekend carpenters. The ceiling grid is mainly 1x2s supported by 2x4 horizontal beams. To make a handy glassware rack, attach 1x2 sections to several members of the grid, spacing them so glassware will hang securely. Position this type of ceiling grid low enough to provide additional storage space above it—and comfortable access to the items up there.

The high-flying ladder shown *above* keeps ski equipment convenient, yet out of the way. To install a ladder, put four hollow wall anchors into the ceiling. Replace the bolts in the anchors with eyebolts big enough for rope to pass through. Screw four screw eyes into the ladder. Run the rope through the eyebolts and thread it through the screw eyes, tying knots to secure the ladder.

UNDER EAVES

Some top-notch storage space may be tucked under the eaves of your house. Because the angles are awkward, the space is often ignored completely. One simple way to use it is to put up a knee wall, add a door or two for access, and make the space into a convenient catch-all. If you're more ambitious, space under the eaves can take on function and flair worthy of any room in your home. Here are a couple of examples.

Low ceilings under the eaves are no drawback in the attic-office shown *above*. A simple, well-designed bookcase of birch plywood nestles under the sloped ceiling. Besides putting reference books within arm's length of the desk, it helps square up the room's proportions. Better yet, the solid-back bookcase is on casters and can easily be rolled out for access to little-

used boxed files that are kept in the lowest section of the eave-space.

Even the telephone makes imaginative use of available space. Its wood stand is ingeniously clamped to a vent pipe, putting it at a convenient angle and leaving comfortable standing room in front of it.

In the top-floor bedroom shown *opposite,* every inch is put to use. Bed, books, clothes, and a menagerie of furry friends are all sheltered close under the roof. Drawers under the bed store large, bulky items, and miniatures nestle in a tiny slice of space over the closet door. Shelves that flank the bed and line the desk alcove provide ample room for books and other treasured belongings.

CLOSE TO
THE HEARTH

Fireplaces in older or traditionally styled homes are often bracketed by built-in bookshelves or display niches. The two fireplaces on these pages take a more contemporary approach to shelf and storage space, using simple lines and innovative design as the basis for carving storage out of spaces that might otherwise have been attractive but underused.

The sleek firewood bins shown on these two pages are a far cry from the strictly utilitarian containers of past generations, but they're no less practical.

The raised hearth that serves as a base for the wood-burning stove shown *above* has the smooth good looks of a cocktail table. In addition, however, there's storage room beneath it for enough split wood to keep the stove going for a long time.

In the fireplace unit shown *opposite*, wood tucks into an open compartment that is surfaced with brick to match the cantilevered hearth. The bin is open on both sides of the fireplace wall to allow for easy loading and unloading.

Keep in mind that the floor of a storage cavity like either of those shown here should be made of a smooth, easy-to-clean, noncombustible surface. The exterior of a fireplace wall or a wall facing a wood stove must be faced with brick, tile, mineral board, or other noncombustible material.

Fireplace plus
The handsome fireplace shown *opposite* is even more useful than it first appears to be. Really a room module, it defines spaces without enclosing them, and houses essential services as well. Here, a fully equipped entertainment center with adjustable shelves for the sound system and records occupies the end section of the unit. And note that even without a fireplace, you can use the module concept to gain extra storage space.

AROUND THE BED

Typical bedroom storage includes dressers, night tables, wardrobes—all good places to keep things, but all space eaters. Another kind of bedroom storage space is available, though, and it may be for you. Customized built-ins around and beneath the bed turn underused areas into first-class storage, conveniently located yet out of sight.

Custom-made built-ins are often the keys to finding storage space where ready-made furniture won't fit or won't look right. The bedrooms pictured here show two versions of the built-in solution.

Walls of compact storage surround the diagonally positioned bed shown *opposite*. Sleek wall units extend from either side of the platform bed, and fabric-covered upper cabinets add still more bedside storage. Handy cubbyholes become caches for reading material, leaving an expanse of open surfaces for decorative accessories and plants. Space under the triangular headboard, accessible by lifting the top, stores extra blankets, pillows, and other items used only occasionally.

The corner-hugging storage collection pictured *below* puts precious bedroom space to efficient use. A narrow table with a flip-down front stores bulky items handily; the drawered nightstand, with its two shelves, adds valuable storage space. And beneath the bed, deep drawers provide the equivalent of an extra bureau.

Bedside manners for storage seekers

If you're thinking of building in some extra bedside storage, here are some general points to keep in mind.
• Make use of space under beds and window benches.
• Add a storage headboard—or a more imaginative equivalent, a table or desk—behind the bed.
• Place cabinets or drawer units beside the bed.
• Consider top cabinets, for still more storage.
• Use easy-care materials for surfaces.

ON THE WALL

Talk about wall storage and what's most likely to come to mind is a series of shelves—or a storage unit backed up against a wall. But wall storage can be much more than that. You can use the wall itself for hanging, storing, and displaying everything from practical objects to purely decorative ones.

Walls are naturals for storage. They're the most expansive vertical surfaces you're likely to have in your house, and they command immediate attention with or without decoration. What you store on walls should be attractive and worthy of that attention.

The tiny section of wall pictured *opposite* is a nostalgic, three-dimensional still life as evocative as any work of art. Wall-mounted shelves and pegs, plus a tabletop and tucked-away basket, provide a backdrop for an arrangement of children's clothing and country-style accents.

Bolder, more dramatic decorative effects highlight the long hallway wall shown *at upper left.* Here, a once-bland white wall houses an impressive array of ethnic art. For this kind of art storage/display to be successful, you need to vary sizes and textures and confine the arrangement to a clear-cut geometric space. Otherwise, the impact will be lost.

Not all wall storage has to be on the walls themselves. Windows, after all, are an integral part of most walls, and they lend themselves to certain types of decorative storage. Fitted with glass shelves, stationary windows, like those pictured *at lower left,* can store favorite accessories and set a mood inside and out at the same time. Because window storage is on view from two sides, arrangement is especially important. Vary heights, colors, textures—and don't crowd the area. As with many other things, a fine line exists between comfortable coziness and crowded clutter.

FROM SOMETHING ELSE

The ability to see everyday items in unusual ways is another key to unlocking new storage space. On these two pages we show a pair of antiques that have been updated to keep pace with changing storage needs. Other good candidates for conversion include iceboxes, dry sinks, pie safes, and armoires, but the list only begins there. With some imagination and ingenuity, you can recycle almost any item into an innovative custom-storage piece.

Storing quilts or memorabilia in a trunk is nothing new—but storing them as decorative items is largely a twentieth-century innovation. The vintage trunk shown *below* was refinished and topped with a sheet of ¼-inch-thick glass. Not only does it provide attractive full-view storage, it's also a useful extra table.

The ornate old cupboard pictured *opposite* is a more ambitious conversion. It houses everything needed for entertaining—including the music. The top half is fitted with adjustable shelves for bottle and glass storage. Three ready-made wine racks placed side by side in the lower portion of the cupboard leave room for stereo equipment on a shelf above.

Here are some general tips for recycling old furniture into new storage.
• If the finish is not in good condition, and cannot be salvaged, start by removing the old finish with paint stripper. You can then leave the piece natural, paint it, or refinish it.
• To protect the new/old storage piece from moisture and spills, give it a couple of coats of polyurethane varnish.
• To allow for ventilation or wiring, replace part of a solid back with perforated hardboard.
• Shine old brass trim; if a piece has iron and steel hardware, darken it with liquid stove blacking.
• Freshen the interior with a decorative layer of wallpaper or fabric.
• A word of warning: If you're dealing with a rare and valuable antique, keep changes to a minimum. They detract from a piece's authenticity and will probably reduce resale value.

WHERE TO GO FOR MORE INFORMATION

BETTER HOMES AND GARDENS® BOOKS

Want to learn more about planning and maximizing storage space at your house? These Better Homes and Gardens® books can help.

Better Homes and Gardens®
NEW DECORATING BOOK
How to translate ideas into workable solutions for every room in your home. Choosing a style; furniture arrangements; windows, walls, and ceilings; floors; lighting; and accessories. 433 color photos, 76 how-to illustrations, 432 pages.

Better Homes and Gardens®
DOLLAR-STRETCHING DECORATING
Save on furnishings and decorating costs without sacrificing style or comfort. Filled with easy-to-carry-out ideas, practical suggestions, do-it-yourself projects, and how-to drawings. 160 color photos, 125 illustrations, 192 pages.

Better Homes and Gardens®
COMPLETE GUIDE TO HOME REPAIR,
MAINTENANCE, & IMPROVEMENT
Inside your home, outside your home, your home's systems, basics you should know. Anatomy and step-by-step drawings illustrate components, tools, techniques, and finishes. 515 how-to techniques; 75 charts; 2,734 illustrations; 552 pages.

Better Homes and Gardens®
COMPLETE GUIDE TO GARDENING
A comprehensive guide for beginners and experienced gardeners. Houseplants, lawns and landscaping, trees and shrubs, greenhouses, insects and diseases. 461 color photos, 434 how-to illustrations, 37 charts, 552 pages.

Better Homes and Gardens®
STEP-BY-STEP BUILDING SERIES
A series of do-it-yourself building books that provides step-by-step illustrations and how-to information for starting and finishing many common construction projects and repair jobs around your house. More than 90 projects and 1,200 illustrations in this series of six 96-page books:
STEP-BY-STEP BASIC PLUMBING
STEP-BY-STEP BASIC WIRING
STEP-BY-STEP BASIC CARPENTRY
STEP-BY-STEP HOUSEHOLD REPAIRS
STEP-BY-STEP MASONRY & CONCRETE
STEP-BY-STEP CABINETS & SHELVES

Other Sources of Information

Most professional associations publish lists of their members, and will be happy to furnish these lists upon request. They also may offer educational material and other information.

American Hardboard Association (AHA)
887-B Wilmette Road
Palatine, IL 60067

American Plywood Association
7011 S. 19th Street
P.O. Box 11700
Tacoma, WA 98411

California Redwood Association
591 Redwood Highway, Suite 3100
Mill Valley, CA 94941

Cellulose Manufacturers Association (CMA)
5908 Columbia Pike
Baileys Crossroads, VA 22041

Gypsum Association
1603 Orrington Avenue
Evanston, IL 60201

National Houseware Manufacturers Association (NHMA)
1130 Merchandise Mart
Chicago, IL 60654

The Stanley Works
Dept. BHG
P.O. Box 1800
New Britain, CT 06050

Western Wood Products Association
1500 Yeon Building
Portland, OR 97204

ACKNOWLEDGMENTS

Architects and Designers

The following is a listing, by page, of the interior designers, architects, and project designers whose work appears in this book.

Pages 8-9
 Philip Smerling
Pages 10-11
 Tony Garrett, Jeff Hicks
Pages 12-13
 Ronald Katz
Pages 14-15
 Leslie John Koeser, American Olean Tile Co.; Larry Walker, Don Olsen Associates
Pages 16-17
 Lawrence Gordon, AIA
Pages 18-19
 Daryl Hansen
Pages 20-21
 John Matthias, California Redwood Association
Pages 48-49
 Stephen Mead
Page 52-53
 Lawrence Gordon, AIA
Pages 54-55
 Philip Tusa Design, Inc.
Pages 74-75
 Stephen Matthias; Donna Warner
Pages 76-77
 Harley-Jensen, AIA; Alan Jones, Waterfront Woodwork Co.
Pages 78-79
 David Immenschuh, IBD, and Patty Berkbile, Nelson Associates Architects, Inc.; Pilgrim/Roy
Pages 80-81
 J. Carson Boaler
Pages 82-83
 Debora K. Reiser; Melvin A. Solomon, AIA, Solomon Claybaugh Young Architects; Sandkraft

Pages 86-87
 Peter Rodi; Virginia Frankel; J. Carson Boaler
Pages 92-93
 Deborah and Jerry Burns
Pages 94-95
 Marilynn Paulson Interiors
Pages 96-97
 Ted and Cynthia Kloss
Pages 100-101
 Mark Haviland
Pages 102-103
 Tony Lisac
Pages 104-105
 Tony Lisac; Sam Gordon; Don Olsen
Pages 108-109
 Suzy Taylor, ASID
Pages 110-111
 Stephen Mead; Don Roberts, Roberts Associates Architects, Planners
Pages 114-115
 James Chapman
Pages 122-123
 Linda Joan Smith
Pages 124-125
 Syd Dunton, Trident Designs, California Redwood Association
Pages 126-127
 Tom Tavernor, American Plywood Association
Pages 128-129
 Robert Sienes, AIA; Julia Lundy Sturdevant, Western Wood Products Association
Pages 130-131
 Marian Miura, American Plywood Association; Thomas L. Thomson
Pages 132-133
 Western Wood Products Association

Pages 134-135
 Arvid Orbeck, American Plywood Association; John Matthias, Chevron/Ortho, California Redwood Association
Pages 136-137
 Robert Engman, AIA, California Redwood Association
Pages 138-139
 Jean Jens
Pages 140-141
 Alex Baer
Pages 142-143
 Georgia Young, Morley Smith
Pages 144-145
 Jerry Ross and Debbie Schmitz
Pages 146-147
 Earling Faick, AIA; Ray Urban & Roger Widmer
Pages 148-149
 Ralph F. Jones, AIA; Paul Peitz, Total Environment Action
Pages 150-151
 Keith Gasser, Jesse Benesch & Associates; Jenny Fitch, R.B. Fitch, Jr.
Pages 152-153
 Bettye Wagner

Manufacturers and Associations

We extend our thanks to the following manufacturers and associations, who contributed materials to this book.

American Olean Tile Company
American Plywood Association
California Redwood Association
Closet Maid System, Clairson International
Heller
The Hirsch Company
Ingrid
Lillian Vernon
The Stanley Works
Western Wood Products Association

Photographers and Illustrators

We extend our thanks to the following photographers and illustrators, whose creative talents and technical skills contributed to this book.

Mike Blaser
Ernest Braun
Ross Chapple
Mike Dieter
Steve Fridge
John Fulker
Karlis Grants
Hellman Design Associates
Bill Helms
William Hopkins
Bill Hopkins, Jr.
Thomas E. Hooper
Armen Kachaturian
Maris/Semel
Steve Marley
E. Alan McGee
Bradley Olman
Charles R. Pearson
Karl Reik
Bob Strode
Jessie Walker

STORAGE

INDEX

Page numbers in *italics* refer to illustrations or illustrated text.

Have BETTER HOMES AND
GARDENS® magazine
delivered to your door.
For information, write to:
MR. ROBERT AUSTIN
P.O. BOX 4536
DES MOINES, IA 50336